Ancestors & Species

Also by Tom Lowenstein:

The Death of Mrs Owl
Eskimo Poems from Canada and Greenland
Filibustering in Samsara
Filibustering in Samsara — A Footnote
The Things That Were Said of Them
Ancient Land: Sacred Whale
Sea Ice Subsistence at Point Hope, Alaska
The Vision of the Buddha
A Social History of Tikigaq, Alaska

Tom Lowenstein

Ancestors and Species

New & Selected
Ethnographic Poetry

Shearsman Books

Exeter

This edition first published in the United Kingdom in 2005 by
Shearsman Books
58 Velwell Road
Exeter EX4 4LD

http://www.shearsman.com/

ISBN 0-907562-74-4

Acknowledgements
The two images on the cover and those on pages 6, 34 and 90 are reproduced
by courtesy of the Trustees of the British Museum, and feature late 18th
and early 19th century ivory engravings by Inupiaq Eskimos of North-West
Alaska.

The poems printed here previously appeared in the following volumes:
Filbustering in Samsara (The Many Press, London, 1987); *Ancient Land:
Sacred Whale* (Bloomsbury, London; Farrar, Strauss & Giroux, New York,
1993; paperback edition, The Harvill Press, London, 2000), to all of which
publishers grateful acknowledgement is made to republish. Passages in Part 3
have appeared in the following magazines: *First Intensity, Great Works* (online),
London Review of Books, Masthead (online), *Shearsman, Skanky Possum*. Many
thanks to all the editors who took these pieces.

The publisher gratefully acknowledges financial assistance from Arts Council
England for its 2005-2007 publishing programme.

CONTENTS

I

Introduction and Note

The poems in this volume have all emerged from ethnographic work in northwest Alaska and come from three separate periods of writing spread over thirty years. I first went to the Arctic in 1973 with the mildly confused intention both of recording traditional stories and writing a long poem in the open field idiom. But the intensity of ethnographic work and the power of the material I encountered in Tikigaq (Point Hope, Alaska), soon put paid to the second ambition. With the exception of *Episode with Hawk and Shaman* which was sketched in situ, everything here was written looking back to Alaska from Europe.

The pieces in Part 1 register three responses to the often confusing impact of the native New World on a non-scholar from Europe who was struggling to comprehend the patterns of widely separated but submerged ancient cultures which seemed obscurely once to have belonged to each other. A note to *Labrys* from 1987, the first poem reprinted here, gives the context of that search:

> Written at Phaistos (Crete) after meeting on the road a woman about to return to the north of England, while I was due back in the Arctic. The poem attempts to explore this woman's sudden absorption into the labyrinth of archaic female history and her consequent meditation. This reaches far beyond her [disingenuous] 'centuries ago', to a quasi-Palaeolithic dream-time whose images nonetheless derive from northwest Alaska and pre-Alaskan Beringia (the Bering Land bridge).

Here I should add in explanation to this poem that the village where I worked lay within the northern zone of what had once been Beringia: that perishingly cold steppe which for thousands of years during the last ice age joined the regions that the Bering Sea would later separate into Europe and the Americas. The small bands of Eurasian tribespeople who later became Native Americans travelled this region and hunted (and perhaps contributed to the extinction of) the Pleistocene mega fauna – steppe bison, woolly rhinoceros, elk and not least the mastodon. The Inuit people with whom I studied had no memory or knowledge of this remote period. The mastodon, which figures in this poem and in *La Tempesta's X-ray*, was known to the Inuit, however, because they often found teeth and tusks in river cliffs and similar mud burials, and they assumed it to have been a giant burrowing rodent. This they called *kiligvak*, a word that entered the human naming system and attached to a man born ca. 1865 and his son (Jimmie Killigivuk) who was my principle informant. From these two circumstances flowed part of my preoccupation with Beringia and the mastodon hunt whose ceremonial elements perhaps paralleled later Inuit brown bear and whale cults. A second unverifiable imagining concerned the power and status of Paleolithic women. Prompted by experience of 20th century Inuit women, I projected a matriarchy (at least a psychological one) onto ice-age women and attributed to them a compendium of cultic and subsistence skills from which they pushed through into the Neolithic. The anonymous woman whom I saw casually leaving the ruins of Phaistos, where the goddess Rhea had been worshipped, is thus dragged back into a labyrinth of time and cultures, to become the poem's narrator, a witness to Old World/New World interrelationships, free-associating over dreamlike spaces of prehistory.

While Beringia lay underfoot, a back country of myth and shamanistic lore possessed the aged mastodon from whom I was learning community traditions. Jimmie Killigivuk (1891-1980) was the oldest man in a rapidly modernising native society, and as he recited stories, sang magical songs and reminisced about his parents' and grandparents' generations, it was as if he peeled the 20th century skin from the village to reveal layers of vaguer and slower strata where the ancestors continued to walk between the old earth and whalebone iglus.

Once I had been working with Jimmie Killigivuk for six months, I too began to experience the composite, historically syncretic nature of local time. Many things happen all at once in this sphere. The myths come alive, the ancestors chatter and intermediate events, such as the arrival of traders and church men in the 19th century, inhabit a fluctuating medium that co-exists within the archaic and the modern. This must be an experience familiar to many historians, and it is what informed both the previously untitled *Shaman Episode* and later, *La Tempesta's X-ray*, with its more diffuse evocation of times and cultures.

Labrys

for Judith Holden

Time in the north had been
  frozen onto a view of the sun
    masking the earth's movement . . .

'So it doesn't matter here,
  these works of ours,' she winces,
    in a deflection of the moon's season,

casting backwards
  into the home city
    a glance of self-disparagement

she will get to grips with
  once the crisis of freedom
    becomes memory smiling

back at her
  through the bricks
    from the forsaken pastoral.

Then to a wall of exotic
  magenta thistles,
    canopied with bee-tone,

she adapts direction,
  faking
    an unused assimilation

as though distance from the ritual habit
  became character, determinant,
    the out-of-body condition:

half an element –
  from the mouth – of her
    issuing in reed striplings

through some whistle
   of a satyr passing,
      the other, memory-stammering . . .

'Centuries ago,'
   she descried to herself,
     'we were half-concerted only

in this language-costume,
   differentiated,
      in a furs condiment.

Then was the chase on
   constant
      to entrap this species

into the contemporary evolution.
   Talking etc.
      was only part of the practice:

the action of a claw,
   a midnight dream-stick,
      cartoned our faces

that were geared to sun masks
   of the upper universe
      wherein beast and spirit mingled,

danced together,

the expression stiffened
   and yet jingled
      between eye-holes

the law gabbing
              on a separable leather . . .

It went with a certain amplitude,
   a boldness, eventually,'
      she cast herself back in it,

'Experimental masculinity,
   goaded as though on tusks
      of quarter moon and mastodon ivory,

into the attack-posture,
   hardening with fire
      a resolution

to affront the inhabited dream-night
   which belittles effort,
      where the other species

are heard prowling
               the inviolate undergrowth . . .

There came then,'
   she considered,
      working the picture,

'*our* elevation – treasure! –
   to minority,
      asphyxiated by exaggerated reverence

(for us
      and itself)

and so came churning
   from the moon's position
      furnishings, we think, of self-preferment:

a stand-up posture maybe:
   solidarity-madness
      (adaptive of some intermediate view

of our equivalence)
   reaching from the arrears
      into a premonitory version:

Thing-person or queen-human
   addressing the question
      to some unresponsive goddess

from the cave-womb progenitrix . . .

The creation went on raving
    sadly into the crepuscular
        without missing us,

the old participation,
    if it meant anything to them
        transformed from species-mandala

into some tighter
                    claw-mingling.

Here was space
    made into the more
        solitary perspective,

'that' created out of 'this'
    or 'this' from the 'other' —
        it could make little difference,

merely there was ascension supposed,
    high-geared in our company
        hallooing the great

crevice of the sky and ocean,
    bird and fish become
        our thrust-quarry,

roasting the god pieces
    of it now and here
        when the supplies dwindled

that our differentiation
    from companion species
        might continue.

Thus we pushed at each other
    to develop – through
        mutual rejection – our resources,

fought the ill-fit dreams back
   untrustworthy though sincere:
      complete relationship

finding its desserts
   within the antagonism of the parts
      that belonged together

while resenting the link-up.

Alternately we worshipped
   One and Many,
      following the great herds of species

until numbers with the ultimate
   were mingled,
      and we mated them

in round-dance, singing,
   then an oak grove, altar flame,
      totemic spirals.

Thought, no:
   it was memory's perfection
      that gave rise to desire

for continuity outwards:
   a loyalty to the old passwords
      in our cave-dwelling

and the misery of darkness
   exalted to a sum
      from which we pressed
                        the blood-line's future . . .

Unlike flowers, it was
   the women jeering into competence
      the flesh-gatherers' journey -

and then sung them babies.
   This was the second meat-arrival,
      delved for in the pit

of death with pleasure
                    or a traditionally inspired joking.

Here was a powerful
   grammar of assistance recognised:
      yet it poured from the centre

remaining the intact momentum:
   courage and fuel,
      and big unanswerable reservoirs of physique

thanked by production
   were the ordinary-careless,
      as snow-weather filed at bone structure

and tedium repaired it
   with long thread's generation
      and the back-sinew's appliqué.

Murmurings – at most
   a curse within the exogamy –
      were at the rear of this weaving.

Action between planets
   took on, true,
      a division of labour quantity:

this group doing the actual flying,
   ours shouting between
      distant surfaces,

since the moon's answer
   was to come in sexualised language
      purifying a man's domination techniques,

since these were not hidden,
   the reward being collective:
      monopoly sustained through

a certain air-twist
   like a knot
      in the communications plasma,

the wind of them
   rattling in vast numbers
      through the ventilation holes

breathed constantly
   consistently, by children
      and the lung's blood
               riddled by its induction.

'*Are* we?', collective,
   as in identity of birth pang: suffering
      which kept us joyful and quiet

at the earliest stages
   which then became habit:
      that underneath-wisdom

like a stick bending
   to an important luggage
      the weight having ostentatious

or ostensible beauty
         without keeping itself suspended . . .

Like a whip-lash, keeping children
   in a circle,
      came the song's induction

between hearth guardians
   where the brooding hovered
      at a foundation, level.

Here was the basis of it all:
   an enduring stain
      of the placenta on tradition

in its blood circle:

official laughter and name-ties
   rounding off the bitter edges
      where death cut in so often and purely.

The fount never ceased pumping
   even when severity had cauterised
     all former outlets

or the cosmos passed into depression:
   antlers of the moon broken,
     and the hunting tackle in pieces.

Spring passed,
   nearly every generation,
     into summer,

and came secret favour-contributions:
   bison losing their tracks
     through the promise of flora,

thundering softly towards our enterprise
   in the joy-will
     of their offering.

Makers and receivers double,
   it was strict accuracy
     and definition

that we scolded the cubs' shape to.
   The bravura of land and water courses,
     each with its fitness,

blazed shape to their
   weapons, and knowledge
     in their mouths and fingers . . .

Now was the weather
   growing vaguer and more complex.
     Heat and darkness

less defined the high theophanies:
   longer onus
     went with smaller separation,

girls of the forage
   having a second kingdom
    to choose from,

and the spirits became brigands
   pirated from the male
    ectoplasm of soul-fire,

mother in her hovel
   counting foggily
    the wearisome changes,

as if blows from the sun's head
   struck hers,
    cancelling the observation.'

Episode with Hawk and Shaman

. . . But it's not merely the surprise of all this beauty which
knocks the heart out of shape – though that's unquestioned –
it's the fact that the dream we entered locks abruptly into
new and bolder focus,
                         and suddenly we understand that this
familiar landscape was vaster and more complex than we could
ever have imagined, and so we upbraid ourselves for
complacently thinking we knew anything yesterday.

And then, just at that moment, when our previous ignorance
seemed so incredible, a second time the vision is translated:
as we sip tea, or so imagine, with a woman on her
veranda,
                  suddenly two men, two messengers, emerge from nowhere –
from a door in the earth, from a cabin in the water – It is a
group of Eskimos approaching cheerfully,
                              and with their
streaming cigarettes they beckon round the corner of an
iglu that we never noticed, as we trudged through the
tundra and over the beach-heads,
                          and with gestures of conspiracy
in their direction – nodding and wagging their heads and
hooking the air with their fingers – they summon us to yet a
new dimension:

And now we're in a space with strangers,
    gazing on a narrow bight of water,
and the earth underfoot is crusted
    with the vertebrae of seal and walrus;
braziers of driftwood flame in a cross wind,
    and the smell of fresh whale oil rises
from the sleeves of our companions.

We stand there chewing meat and blubber,
    tossing the dogs rib-bones,
joy-locked with the sheer intensity
    of this sudden interruption:
it is radiant and complex to the senses,
    and yet how simply it completes things!

A lever is flicked down in the subconscious,
   and all the useless erudition of a lifetime
is flushed out and recycled in the tug of prana . . .

   There we were, slogging across the north wind on a sandbar
feet sinking backwards in recalcitrant loose shingle
   getting nowhere, caught like a fish
in the reticulations of the air currents
   which had dehydrated and exhausted us.
Now the same wind, blasting the house corners
   and tearing horizontally the long bright grasses,
plays before the eyes like a spirit in a separate vision:
   as though on a screen, harmless and distant as the sky,
through which clouds and geese and Pintail ducks are swarming.
   And there's no occasion to applaud yourself for
standing here with your new companions who have drawn you
   with no special purpose, to their camp-place,
to ruminate quietly on your change of position,
   to watch the wind paddling away violently
at the fluctuating landscape and to realise with a heightened clarity
   that *you* were there a moment previously, and that
there it continues, with only the participation of your seeing
   and that it is real, and you are real also.

A hawk rises, a white spot on its tail,
   and loiters in a circle round some willow bushes;
then there is a flock of plovers in a broad skein of seven
   flying inland from the sea, and they circumnavigate
the predator for fear of invasion.

   Suddenly you realise that the young man standing near you is a shaman.
"*Iirigii! Angatkuq ilvin!* (You're a shaman. I am frightened!)"
   you murmur speaking in Eskimo,
with its uvular stops and slashed l's
   and its long linked polysynchretic organization of morphemes,
stringing together, as you continue, the intricate tackle of the language,
   like a sequence of bound fish hooks
to their baleen and sinew leaders:
   the beautifully ordered verb-endings and intransitives
crackle on your tongue, feeding themselves down from their sparks
   into you, until the thorax is illuminated by the
contraption of the entire grammar, ablaze with its connective logic.

19

The young *angatkuq* stands gazing at the plovers.

"I wonder what it's like, right now," he mutters,
   "up there cheeping in the broad heaven?"
And at once his mind is flocked up with the migrants,
   dissolving his bones in a wide airy circle,
leaving his skin with us.
   "It is *they* who have come to investigate *me*",
you realize after a slow interval,
   "setting their camp-house in my path
in the knowledge that I would discover them."
   Now the older man launches into *unipkaaq*, a spirit story,
in an outlandish dialect from the northern sea-coast.
   A shaman mother has been re-assimilating all her children
through the holes in her back, and only the last child
   eventually succeeds in plugging them, and so himself becomes a shaman.
It is a long telling, and successively inflexions of the situation
   get more twisted. You glance at your watch. It is four in the morning.
"Time for you to go, *ha?*" motions the young shaman,
   indicating a vague corner of the *iglu*,
and you slip beyond it, without speaking, onto the horizon.

La Tempesta's X-Ray

Gleizes, no,

        Soulages, perhaps, working his great house brush

in a war-shadow,

           consolidating, partially, the split head of

its taper,

       panels a gray canvas of the twilight's negative, and

spreads –

       like the crushed particles of some used match-heads

rubbed on

       cartridge paper – out in broad charcoally flanks

                         a ragged

honeycomb of fretwork, light-charred,

              flawed with excrements

of lunar interstices

        (crumbled nightwhale jointed into vertebrae

of chiaroscuro . . .)

         It is a dull, peppery view: a montage,

at once,

     in colonnades of basalt, and husky-cubed, industrial

                    contraptions

latent, half-illumined in refrigerated alcoves

             against Jacobean panelling.

For here in this monochromatic chancel

          of bi-tones, are no complicated

Grinling Gibbonses of

      trumpetwork and oak leaf scrolls

and acanthus,

    but rather, yes, there is an austere rectilinearity of conduits,

leading one

    into another nowhere,

          like the sewer blueprint for a city

of minds on the high-rise
                             that have long been stopped-up,
and are still too hygienic
                             to have made use of the system,
leaving it 'clean' also.
                                  Here then through our round
free-flying dream of
                       cromatismo, it is the uprights and the
laterals invading —
                       a labour-force of ghostlike neolithic masons
                                              drafted
into the Magdalenian cave sanctuaries
                                where the beasts are a-tumble
through their sacred positions:
                         weightless oxen superimposed on
or gestating in the translucent
                         wombs of ancient horses float here:
stag, deer, mastodon, rhinoceros
                             and ibex browse adrift and shudder
and gallop in the fold-bellied
                       gravity of tertiary limestone passages —
and then, just once, it appears,
                       like a visionary warning from the finger
of some ancient child cartoonist:
                       that singular
lank shaman-figure,
                 a scrawny rectangle,
rigid in trance, bird-mask
                       and clawlike erection swooned lame
against
        the rounded girth-energy of a bison
                             who's transected

by the other straight thing,

and who thus relieves himself of

the bag of his entrails ———

The machine is in action, all right:

'Man' recognising innerly

the perspective of his outward measurement,

his vertebral force,

the weakness and necessity of perpendiculars,

the ambiguity

of a self-made or self-styling right angle ——————————

It was coming and it has triumphed,

technic uniformity

in all its dangers and loveliness

flowering in ziggurat and pyramid societies. . .

But then wasn't it the old Pharaonic kingdom
which finally entrenched the vigour
of this rectilinear conceit within our cosmos?

Think of the sky's Djed-supports assembling,
the straight-backed Ibis scribe,
    the resurrection of Osiris ———
           primeval stems of lotus
    pushing between underworld and sunlight,
                     rearing serpents ———
I dream of warm brown silhouettes of hunters
    upright in the papyrus marshes
raising a multitude of slanting water-fowl
    into the pruinescence of that Nilotic dawn-burst.

       Yes, and I have witnessed something
of this process' evolution,
       from the sea ice, one sullen mid-February
afternoon in the Arctic:
       the village of Tikigaq in a stubble of
nineteenth-century whalebone
        rising over the northernmost pressure-ridges
of the 68th parallel,
      like the lower mandible of a Pleistocene
fish-jaw
    meeting the half-moon's edge, as the liquified brass
                of the
sun's blood-fringe descended —

                    The snow swept a rough cerement

over the domed

                    old uninhabited *iglu* dunes

                                        where everything

has had a curve in it at some point

                                (shamans rolling up

the driftwood floor planks

                        and letting them spring back again and so on) —

And then suddenly, blazing upright

                                as though to cast its spectre

over the placid rink of perfectly

                        level *siquliaq* (young thin ice)

stretched out

                gray as the sky's anaesthetic cataract,

                                                and

barnacled with sugar-snow on which bear tracks visible

                                        had slurred

their seaward passage to some breathing holes —

                                        There

stood shining and deranged

                        the city of the future, inland,

Tikigaq, or Tikigatchiaq ('new-Tikigaq')

                                in white/blue razzle

mirage substance, not trembling

                        as in northern summer heat haze,

but frozen on the air,

                like shark-skin tinted

                                sheeny freezer wrapping,

storey upon storey of prefabricated office-space

                                and municipal housing,

arrayed in a cross-hatching of

                        crane necks and derricks,

the time-vandalised multiple elongation of dwellings

                                               a vague,

run in the air meta-city

                   on the latitude of the Standard Oil building

in Chicago:

             unusable high-wind sun-balconies

                          cluttered with

transport damaged condominium accessories —

                           It leapt, yes,

as does Las Vegas out of a basin

                in the Mohave desert at nightfall,

or Denver glazed suddenly

             against the Rockies from an aircraft cabin,

and like those centres,

        Tikigaq upstretching

               on exchange of metals.

    And scraping the slack jello

  of overt appearances,

           with grinding canines,

  ice and granite,

       back, back,

molars churning,

        giant blue/green glacial jawbones

masticate and thunder,

  to leave detritus of Arctic trash town
on post-glaciation Adriatic:
  lead town, *Geld* town,
town of copper west of the Rockies,
  nitrate, *ashlag* and asbestos ghost town,
megaliths of spirit-ice, platonic mica-gneiss dishevelled,
  granite's incandescent sinew streaking ruined edges,
luminous diagonals, alive striations, burning fibulae and tendons,
  light-sludge, silt of darkness' inter-osseous agglutinations

severed from the cartilage and fascia, phosphorescent,
    burning in the rays' dissection,
the final earth form scoured
                          from glaciated carnage,
    chaos junketed in shafts of curfew,
hamstrung in repeated jumble of the two dimensions —

And the city in the flat plate of the pastoral
    is the blueprint – wandering platonic –
of Manhattan, Dresden, Coventry, Southampton, Mestre, West Berlin,
    contemporary London
    bel paese! — unified already.
There it is, by Jack,
    raising its vast sunless concrete ectoplasm in the brown-out,
the cold prefabricated stanchions of the future
    rearing their anticipated, sheetlike femurs,
flesh stripped in the ice masque —

And the dancing pageants
    of Detroit and Harlem
like government-bombed Druid menhirs
    tango through the twilit asphodel
in an auroral Hadean sub-storm,
    with only an attenuated flange,
a bee sting of the *éclaircissement* among the cloud scrapings:

the whole sky rubble like some disastrously planned
    B.I.A-ruined Eskimo village of the late 1990s
reflected upside-down in polished sea ice catastrophe
    on televised ultraviolet microwave 'art' vision.
These are the things when the past is so violent:
    there is a kind of peace about looking into it
like a truce between the souls of materialists
    who have suddenly transcended the infrastructure –
so they imagined it – of their agon.

Thus we see dawn rising
                          on disasters that are ahead of us:
perking like an orange and brown Fanta and coffee solution
into the inverted corneal umbrella-hood of its solitary,
gazing Ruskinesque spectator who is annotating changes in

the cloud formations,
                        aware, rueful, of those spectres
that are to have arisen in the furore of the future
pluperfect, inherent as they must be in the burning molecules
of its foetus.
              The storm is in the looking
                and from looking floods out
                                    knowing innocence.

              And moving down the bank of a river
                    in the strange intersection
          between all this and what's to come,
                    is a solitary female bather,
          who has cast aside her garment by the ruins
                    and neatly steps through short thick grass
          and the dew-laden forget-me-nots
                    towards the ablutions of her childhood.

          Unconscious of the maelstrom
                    – since without surfaces and lightning
          there can be no maelstrom –
                    she treads without wariness or circumspection
          into her enjoyment, which is daily and usual.

Neither neoclassicism nor expressionism have yet occurred
this time, in spite of the aforesaid, all-embracing contiguity
of Armageddon: and though the shadow of our soldier hovers
like a darkly burning pre-aborted seraph across her nudity,

   still the light slides sweetly up her lower thigh
and onto her right shoulder:
   and the face, although blackened
by the very ray that lights it
   slants gracefully away from heaven,
half bent in discretion
   to the cleansing stream water
                              and she's
beautiful and certain as the goddess Flora in April.

   No man covers her with his
                              nor sees her body,
which is more naked in this *pentimento*
   than any fully 'revealed' nude,
such as the woman in *Le Déjeuner sur l'herbe* of Manet,
   whose nakedness is partly a reflection
of the fabric of her dandies' luncheon clothing.

Here she steps
              under the paint,
into the continuous and inconclusive plunge
   of an invisible left thigh
displacing the deep stream water, and dandling
   the surface ripples with the fingers of her right hand.

How beautiful this is at secret morning,
   and so out in the open:
and yet nothing is artless or 'natural' about it
   in the way we like to think old scenes like this are beatific:

No, it is beautiful because it is both eternal
   and without context, brusquely fresh,
and still for ever covered over,
   delectably pleasant for its quietness in the mist,
                                        yet

perhaps almost stultifyingly routine to contemplate the
reality of, and nothing to be ooh-ed and ah-ed at for its
pastoral ingenuousness.

        And thus I am prompted in my softness
to imagine:
        No, there is little to dislike for being ugly in
this world: only there are certain minds that somehow seek
out squalor from in the cavities of their own repression and
project this without caring. How feckless, distant seem the
city rulers!

        But now here in this skinny-dipping
                    instant
    of pure light illumined
            air and water,
    of no-consciousness
        and no no-consciousness,
    the grass stems bend down
          on the paler
    green forget-me-not branches
    and the foot-blade of the bather wavers
    without spilling dew
        or crushing out odour
    into the roscid marjoram thicket.

    It is finished as soon as it is started,
and though in the darkest panel
    of this flat fane of monotones,
our gypsy maid madonna,
    undressed out of flesh's luxury
sits cramped cold
    like a spinster on a Flemish shale slide,
her arms and legs beneath the ray gun
    a cat's cradle of half-freezing bandages of linen,
bone sticks crossing in the livid exhumation,
    she is not of this scene:
she's elsewhere in *Tempesta's* X-ray,
    the bather doubly alone and lovely
in a happy calming –
    like the misprint of a spirit
in the body of some wicked despot –

she's slipped unnoticed into our existence,
salving, if not healing our sharp longing for identities
    beyond the skeleton,
because we do not, can not genuinely see her,
    and may simply know of her

                                persistent contiguity.

                    *

Notes to *La Tempesta's X-ray*

La Tempesta and the X-ray photo

The x-ray poem comes from the middle of a sequence prompted by Giorgione's painting which I saw in the Venice Accademia a few days after returning from field work in 1978. Giorgione was a mystical painter, and this pastoral showing two figures in a symbolically configured but semi-naturalistic landscape represents one of the great mysteries of Renaissance art. Much of Giorgione's work baffled his contemporaries. Vasari commented on frescoes commissioned for the Fondaco dei Tedeschi (now lost): 'I do not understand them, nor have I found any one who did.' Much the same has been said about La Tempesta, of which Kenneth Clark wrote: 'No one knows what it represents; even Michiel, writing in Giorgione's day, could offer no better title than "a soldier and a gypsy"' (Landscape into Art, 1949). Edgar Wind deciphered the symbolism ('Giorgione's Tempesta', Oxford 1969) by identifying the tranquil, detached figures as Fortezza and Carita, while the storm breaking above a city in the background emblematised 'capricious Fortune' which the allegorical figures have transcended. Returning as I just had from an ancient Arctic community where archaic time seemed in constant interplay with the rush of new American currents, I sensed also that the canvas communicated a fragment, or even a continuum, of non-historical time in which the man and woman, like secondary characters in some unidentifiable myth, were contemplatively suspended. History, suggested by quasi-classical ruins, accompanied, without impinging on, their tranquil meditation: a vast sweep of paradoxical experience being thereby suggested. Behind this convergence of timeless arrest and historical vicissitude lay the suggestion of a further Platonic life.

In 1939, an X-ray photograph revealed that the soldier is a *pentimento* of a second nude woman, poised to bathe in the river. The X-ray also exposes a background of rectilinear forms suggestive to me at the time of writing of a twentieth century city landscape. Just as the naked woman prefigures the soldier, so the pastoral is a curtain behind which our own time waits. This notion is linked to the Hindu view, in which inconceivably vast stretches of time are endlessly repeated, the 'past' thus coming before and after the present, and the latter containing both past and future in a constant process of mutual overlay.

Albert Gleizes, 1881-1953, French cubist.

Pierre Soulages, b.1919, French painter of dense black-brushed abstracts.

Grinling Gibbons, 1648-1721, English decorative carver.

cromatismo: the technique of shading with colour, used by Giovanni Bellini, Giorgione and Titian.

'it is the uprights. . .': for some of the thought in this passage, I am indebted to S. Giedion's *The Eternal Present: The Beginnings of Art* (Princeton University Press, 1957).

shaman figure: this is one of the very few human figures in Aurignacian and Magdalenian cave art; it is in the crypt at Lascaux.

Djed supports : 'The idea of the Djed column is that it stands firmly upright — for to be upright is to be alive . . . When the Djed is upright it implies that life will go on in the world.' R.T. Rundle Clark, *Myth and Symbol in Ancient Egypt*, Thames and Hudson, 1959.

Tikigaq (pronounced Tik-eh-raq): an Eskimo village in northwest Alaska. Eskimos living in iglus constructed from turf, driftwood and whale-bone over the past two millenia now live here in American-style dwellings. The nineteenth century whale-bones are the ruins of the last aboriginal dwellings. A pressure ridge is a long spine of heaped sea ice, created by the movement of wind and current.

ashlag : Hebrew for potash, which is extracted from the Dead Sea.

B.I.A. : Bureau of Indian Affairs, a U.S. government agency.

Déjeuner sur l'herbe : Giorgione's *Concert champêtre* in the Louvre, was the source for this painting.

Castelfranco: Giorgione's birthplace.

II

from *Ancient Land : Sacred Whale*

Introduction

The opening fifty pages of the whole book consist largely of prose essays about the form of the peninsula settled by the Tikigaq Inuit and the topographic and mythological relationship of this low-lying sand spit to the annual whale hunt during the pre-contact period. Part Two of the volume, The Ritual Year, surveys Tikigaq's ceremonial and subsistence life through the seasons, and contains prose, translated stories, explanatory dialogues between two fictional Inuit commentators and passages of my own poetry. One theme explored in both parts of the book is the symbolism of duality, and the alternatingly indented verse lines in Part 2 are intended to express this mutually supportive framework of twoness. The quite long and often artefactually packed lines are likewise intended as verbal equivalents of Inuit tools, in particular multiply articulated objects such as harpoons, traps, fishing tackle and the elaborately reticulated different kinds of net used for catching fish, belukha dolphin and seal. The word 'tackle', whose use in Hopkins's 'their gear and tackle and trim' (Pied Beauty) influenced me, occurs in a number of places in these passages, and the hard consonants of that noun are repeated and dispersed through other combinations. My attempt in this regard was to make lines that spoke and enacted the construction of artefacts which in themselves were composite. A harpoon for example, the most complicated of Inuit hand-held weapons, consisted of a variable selection of animal parts (bone, antler, sinew, ivory, skin line, baleen) with a stone point at one extreme and a driftwood pole at the other. The connective/disconnective process of constructing and deploying this (it disassembled on impact) was an aspect of what all hunting weapons were built to achieve. Propelled through space it brought, through a process of extension and contraction, the animal body towards people who then consumed it, in part so as to repeat the process. Another aspect of this pattern was expressed by hundreds of Inuit string games (cat's cradles). In these, space, violence and comic inter-species encounters – as evoked in a description of the autumn games below – are given a metaphysical, often frightening representation. For a longer account of this mimetic creativity see Ancient Land, Notes: II.3.

The subsistence weapon and the playfully spiritualised string game were parts of a social, material and metaphysical world which was, like an animal, itself composed of multiply interconnected joints and ligatures. The jointed together essays, stories and poetry of Ancient Land represent an attempt to evoke this, while within its limited participating sphere, the poetry attempted its own performance of the same. A note on the sources to the complete volume made a further point which is worth repeating:

> My effort has been to reconstruct an old [sacred] drama and to show how people lived within the structure of its poetic idea. Every ritual or subsistence act is a part of the 'poem' within whose sphere the community lived. Local stories embody their own poetry. My own contribution is simply an attempt to encapsulate or interpret in a Western idiom experience which may lie under or parallel to the narrative genre.

The poems in this selection are thus extracts from my attempt to evoke this cosmos whose interior is represented by lines of poetry which function to lash together and encapsulate detail whose oneness is generally composite and often unstable.

1. Summer

The scene having been introduced by the two fictional narrators, Samaruna and Asatchaq, these passages evoke the weeks between mid-June and September when Tikigaq's population leaves the village and spreads across the territory. While the majority hunt, the mesmerising twenty-four-hour daylight becomes a medium in which young men succumb to visionary experience. Orphan boys, whose solitude and destitution leads them to shamanistic careers, are first described as part of a grandmother's storytelling and then in a longer description of shamanistic initiation.

Summer is the season of emergence and movement. The sun is high; the sea-ice drifts off; whaling is over; the wind comes from the south, and the animals move with it.

While the whales were running they filled the minds of Tikigaq hunters. As spring turns to summer the world comes alive with smaller species.

Eider duck, old squaw, harlequin and scoters pour north to breed in the marshes and wetlands. Guillemots home in on their nesting ledges. Gulls and kittiwakes crowd back with them.

Geese and cranes wing through in V-formation. Eagles and falcons nest on river bluffs and sea cliffs. Plovers and whimbrel, snipe and phalarope raise their young on the coast and the tundra. Owls hunt in the midnight sunshine.

As soon as the whale hunt and the whaling feast are over the whole village moves out to the south shore to hunt ugruk (bearded seal) and walrus.

Ugruk and walrus have just come north, and hunters stalk them as they bask on the ice-floes. Every umialik needs sealskin to cover his boat-frame for next year's whale hunt. The dark meat, dried and then soaked in seal oil, is eaten all summer.

So while the south wind blows and the sun is high, Tikigaq decamps:
    each family to its place where the ancestors hunted:
tents – used boatskins patched with caribou –
    standing high on the beach-head in the long spring grasses.

Here, among the vertebrae and hip-bones from old seal hunts,
    and the poppies, saxifrage, anemones and willowherb
that have pushed through the tundra between stones and driftwood,
    the women sew their families' gut-skin parkas

and the waterproof boots they'll need all summer.
    And the old have come out, after winter in their iglus:
the men weaving fish nets, women braiding strands of sinew,
    while children, barefoot, chase squirrels and longspurs:

'Sigirik! Sigiriiraq!
Come out little parka squirrel!'
'Qupaluk! Qupaluk!
Qain Qupaluuraq!
And you, little longspur!'

Flubbering their lips, they whistle and banter with the species
    that came out or migrated with the final bowhead,
running through the night sun, only sleeping in the skin tent
    when the women's south-shore stories reach them.

'This is the path,' the grandmother finishes,
    brushing a hand along the south beach [*nali*],
'poor boys, back then, took on journeys to seek visions.
    No one knows where those orphans came from:
whether they were really people, and what animals helped them.
    They started at nali: in dogskins, no boots, hungry:
walking alone, and sleeping with the owls and ptarmigan.
    At Imnat, they met spirits who forced them to play games –
challenged them to dance and wrestle,
    run up the cliffs with whales on their backs –
who made traps with bones and axes and whose songs made them
        dizzy.
    They met brown bears and wolves that hunted them in circles.
They were eaten and coughed back; they became great shamans.
    They walked on. They found uiluaqtaqs on the tundra,
who hunted with their combs, and had teeth in their *utchuks*.
    Any poor boy who had *qilya* [shaman power] beat the spirits at
        their own games,
turned the traps on their owners and stole them as amulets,
    harpooned and married the women who attacked them,
and walked home at snow-fall, to sleep till whaling . . .'

Below, where the beach meets the sea-ice,
    dog-sleds travel, carrying meat to umialiks' caches.
Hunters steer between the ice-floes,

moor their kayaks, track, crawl, spring out and harpoon
the sleeping ugruk, call for their partners,
tow carcasses behind their kayaks, while the hunter who has struck,
cries out to his wife in the voice of the animal
whose spirit helps him and whose amulet he carries.
The women cry back from their tents across the sea-ice,
walk down, sharpening their knives, help drag the seal in,
butcher it, and peg the scraped skin on the tundra.

TIKIGAQ TRAVELLERS

When the ice has drifted and there's open water,
it is time to travel.
The old people stay on shore or pitch their tents in Tikigaq,
where they'll fish, and raid duck nests,
net sea-trout from the beaches, and walk inland to pick berries.

Now the skinboats are loaded with nets, harpoons and ugruk rope,
bags of seal oil, baleen, ivory and whale meat;
the men run the prow across the beach shelf, leap in to their benches,
cram the children between women, puppies, harness, tent skins,
and finally the steersman, the umialik, thrusts off with his paddle,
and the dogs on shore are scolded into hauling by the woman
who runs with them,
as the crew heads down-coast across surf and current.

Before Imnat, they come in, visit kinsfolk's places, qalgi partners,
eat, sit with legs stretched, dry their parkas,
watch the guillemots' low feeding lines fly out for the horizon,
study the grey whale, offshore, and the orca ['sea wolf'] hunting,
back-fin, like the moon, scrawled grey, that signifies inua.
The women shout, as the orca feed, in clouds of seal blood,
'Leave some for me!' they call to its inua,
and run through the water, laughing, to grab lumps of blubber.
At Pinuatchiaq, they stop to scan the marshes from the high ground,
and the sky at Imnat – if the cliffs are swollen there will be good
weather –
then straight on to Isuk, where the flat land meets the first cliffs,
and the beach is cut by running water.
They camp here, drink, eat whaleskin and ugruk, listen to the guillemot
– a bird with no soul because there are too many –

39

and whoop back *'Arru! Arru!'* to them:
massed cries pierced by kittiwakes and ravens.

Next they take the boats round, and land at Sisu where the cliffs are
        ruined.
    The men climb the scree until they reach the nesting ledges,
scale knots and fissures, hang from their fingers,
    clouds of birds rise, showering them with faeces,
the men stuffing eggs in their parka bellies,
    for the women to boil over beach-fires at Isuk,
while those who felt giddy when they first tried climbing,
    walk up the west side, and let rope out for their partners,
who dangle from the cliff-top to scoop birds with pole-nets.

Samaruna said:
Two men, they say, in an ancestor story,
who shared their wives,
were hunting at Imnat
as they always did in partnership.
And the one on the cliff-top let his partner down,
and then untied the rope that held him.
'Stay down and die!' he shouted,
'I'm taking your woman!'

The man on the cliff hung on all summer,
eating guillemots' and gulls' eggs.
When skinboats passed,
his shouts were drowned by wind and sea-birds.
But round his neck, the man wore an amulet,
a brown-bear-snout amulet,
and one night, he took the bear's snout
and chewed it, to liven it with his saliva.
Soon enough he heard a voice above him.
Somebody was calling him.
'Here's rope for you! Climb!
Your wife and partner have gone home already.
Grab this and climb!'
The man tied the rope round his waist.
He reached the cliff-top.
There was a brown bear, his amulet animal.
The bear had lowered its intestines and pulled the man up with them.

The bear said:
'Here I am: your *tupitkaq, your aanguaq,* your *anatkuq.*
That's why I've saved you.'
The bear left for the hills,
and the man walked back to Tikigaq.
He found his wife, and killed his partner.
He'd become a shaman.

The travellers go round the cliffs and past the land controlled by Tikigaq.
They hunt all the way, and cache what they'll need in late summer or
autumn. Slowly they move on to the trade fair at Sisualik, a sand spit a
hundred and thirty miles south of Tikigaq.

At Sisualik they meet southern Inupiaqs, inland river hunters, island
people. Maritime travellers bring whale meat, sealmeat, blubber, ugruk
skins and ivory. Inlanders bring black-bear meat, dried salmon, caribou
and furs from the mammals of the river valleys: fawn skins, marten,
muskrat, red and cross fox, wolf, wolverine and lynx. For three weeks of
July and August hundreds of families camp in small village compounds,
hunting belukha, exchanging goods with inherited partners, and forging
new contacts.

The high ground on the spit is thick with berries, and beyond the
lines of skinboats, tents and kayaks, the villagers hold races and games
of endurance; there are contests between shamans, spouse exchanges,
dances, storytellings, while strangers from the far side arrive quietly,
barter reindeer pelts, glass beads, copper and tobacco for Inupiaq goods
and then leave quickly.

> The poor, who have no skinboats, travel east on foot,
>   in bands, where the caribou take them,
> children in their mothers' parkas, dogs with the tent-skins, poles
>   and side packs.
>   Behind the cliffs, they climb the hill-tops –
> flints and fossil-coral grinding their boot-soles –
>   walking north-east for the valleys where the game feeds,
> setting traps for wolf, fox, marmot, lynx and wolverine.

> Over the hill, they hear loons on the river,
>   watch peregrines hunt from the bluffs of Kuukpak,
> below, through mosquitoes, the tundra stretches, brown and purple,
>   ravens quarrelling with foxes over caribou the wolves have taken,
> the half-sunk antlers' rib-spread arched in hunger,
>   wind rushing through them.

The men stalk, singing *taqsiun* [lure songs]: 'Qa-in! Approach!
                Qa-in! Qa-in!'
    herd the caribou through lakes and rivers
where they chase them in kayaks; line migration tracks
    with cairns and drive them into gulleys.
Eating and drying out the meat all night at sunlit hill camps,
    they skirt the routes their enemies have taken,
and the graves of murdered children whose teeth they hear grinding.
Then there is the outcast, poor boy,
    who was thrown away, and lived with the dogs in ruined iglus,
and who travels alone, to return as a shaman.
    The outcast walks hungry. The wind cuts his parka;
his boots rot in the marshes. The dream from his mind extends
    to where the sky meets tundra, waking vision, never sleeping
while the daylight fills his body,
    sky pours through the sutures and the eye-holes, thorax hollows,
and he sees his skeleton, ablaze and freezing, numbering the bones,
            knows them,
    calling each by name until it sings its answer,
identifies the life-souls clustered at the joints and organs,
    tastes self-meat, comprehending it has died, continues living:
same, no different from companion species,
    and he lies down with the ptarmigan and foxes:
intercourse and inanition: thighs smeared with feathers,
    fox eats his tongue, eyes, heart and liver,
bird-wife escapes with his usuk and testes:
    dog-mother history vomited on stream-bed,
dry with vertebrae, and amulets the moon excreted.

The animals take pity, and undo his ligaments,
    the guts are dried and knotted around tundra hummocks,
jerked towards the light by raven, into winter by the peregrine,
    scavenging his colon, they peck and trample,
leaving the skin empty and his mind in a circle.

Another, destitute, leaves Tikigaq: abandons his weapons,
    joins the wolves, and learns to speak their language,
runs all summer with them, along rivers, with the lame and pregnant,
    eating rodents and foxes, takes a wife among them, a young woman,
who fucks and then eats him.
    Then the wolf umialik calls him and approaches,

butts his wolf skull on the tundra,
  scrapes back the wolf-mask, showing his inua,
the round face-disc, nameless person-spirit, naked, radiant, saying:

'You humans, who have seen us become human, animals
  and human, who have lived with us and shared our food,
who have wives among our people and who know our children:
  you who have come, you'll return to your own people,
and with what you have seen, invite the wolf soul
  to your rituals and dances, so those first times – separated from us
when humans were animals and animals were people –
  are made whole in your story, when you tell them what your
                                                dream was.

'Go back now. You are one of us. Because of your visit,
  you have made us happy. You have joined us. Thank you.
When you were a child, and had no kin, your hunger drove you
                                                from the village.
  Now you are a shaman. You will tell your people how to treat us.
Whenever you sing, you'll remember your wife and your kinsmen
                                                among us.
  And when you hunt the whale in spring, we will help you.

'All this, because you have visited our people.
  But don't be like those other shamans who come once and then
        leave us
and say nothing, leave the story broken, and forget to revisit us.'

The soft, thick hood slips back and the wolf umialik vanishes.
  Home in Tikigaq, the young shaman sleeps all winter:
mind curled in the earth-wound,
  dreams of whale's flukes breaching in the iglu.
They'll catch whales next season.

These journeys took place in the single two-month day of summer, whose warmer weather and unbounded space, with no sunsets or divisions, offered temporary freedom, both of movement and from social pressure.

Isolated in extended families on the tundra and the beaches, people escaped the tensions of the village: the malice of neighbours, jealous rivals,

shame and failure, inherited feuds, and, not least, angry shamans
inadvertently offended whose retribution they continually expected.

So in summer they went out. They were out:
    dropped ritual trappings and taboo imperatives.
Absolved from the absolute and lunar inspection,
    they left at home those forms which,
like the string games patterning their stories,
    implicated a commitment to high communal projects.
So now, the whale hunt over and the moon in abeyance,
    summer was pragmatic, secular, the dream agnostic.

2. Autumn: Myths and Histories

These extracts come from a longer description of ceremonial house activity in the autumn. While the women prepare food and winter clothes in the domestic iglus, the men gather in their qalgis (ceremonial houses) to tell stories, compete in athletic games, exchange gifts, dance and hold shamanistic séances.

> *Samaruna said:*
> The sun goes round.
> It's come round from the north.
> It's circled Tikigaq
> all spring and summer.
> Now the sun goes round,
> it touches the Point,
> and goes down through the sea
> on the western horizon.

> *Asatchaq:*
> It goes south in the winter,
> to where the whales live.
> Next spring it returns
> with the migrant animals.

When the sun went down and the moon lit the twilight, the men swept up their work and pushed it underneath the benches.

Now the sun had touched the Point, the old men started talking. The old men, who had been sleeping or singing and fixing their drum heads, started to tell stories, and the qalgi rituals started.

> *Asatchaq:*
> The old men have their places.
> They sit on their benches
> in the middle of the qalgi.
> The old men sit.
> Their work is finished.
> They do nothing.

> *Samaruna:*
> The old men are frightening.
> What they know is powerful:

what they know has qilya and is qilya:
songs and stories gathered
in them over many winters.

If anyone offends old men,
withholds meat and keeps it hidden,
walks past the old men without their permission:
that man may have to wait,
but his punishment comes later:
a hand, a leg or the belly will swell,
his fingers will grow numb
when he fixes his bow string,
the ice will crack,
in fair weather, and maroon him:
in its time, this will come,
because old men have qilya.

Asatchaq:
Their songs travel and attack the body.
Their stories have qilya.
What happened in the past
lives on in stones.
They use this like shamans.
Old men are shamans.

For the old have survived, by skill and luck manipulated
    through lives long enough to validate the knowledge
they inherited from elders who, themselves from elders,
    learned to tackle and survive extreme conditions:
each near-impossibility converted to procedure and tactic:

threading *ways* through sea-ice for their seal and bear meat,
    with the acquisition, on each safe return with meat, of knowledge:
the path of each journey, worked in with the knowledge pattern,
    passed vertically down kin lines, and spread through the qalgis.

What the old men knew and taught were knowledge systems
    which had power, qilya, and exerted qilya:
and these were deployed against energies
    that made life dangerous and unpleasant:

high wind and currents, snow-drift, blizzards,
    rivers impassable or too shallow to navigate,
high seas, winter darkness, summer marsh lands and mosquitoes,
    rough capes, hunting in famine through vast empty tundra,
walking tangled shifting sea-ice, kayaking through young mush,
    dragging animals up-wind over sea-ice through the darkness,
hunting polar bear and brown bear, great souls, dangerous,
    whose skins torn, meat ingested, shades placated,
demanded expeditions, expiation, and their repetition:

these – the totality, at each angle preying on the hunter's body,
    assaulting what the mind deflected or was bent to –
were daily confronted by Tikigaq hunters;
    and generated, by their opposition, means, skill and qilya:

an elaborated system, matching, formal counter-construct
    transmitted by example and in stories.
On account of what they'd known and told, and therefore given,
    the ancestors were complete and perfect:
and the living, who inherited the forebears' name souls,
    were a partial incarnation of these namesakes.

But the living were faced daily with ordeals
    revealing human imperfection,
and so they faltered, they thought, badly.
    Divided between present and ancestral selves,
the discord made the makeshift of the present seem a failure,
    and this bound them closer to the elders' precepts.

Halfway towards ancestral status, their hunting finished,
    with a knowledge of the dead that they alone remembered,
the elders, too, were sacred:
    and the stories they recited every autumn formed a web that
            united past and present,
and sacralised the present before winter started.

So in autumn, the old men started to tell stories.
    All that evening, when the sun touched the Point,
and next day, and the nights and days that followed,
    they told Tikigaq's stories,
tying everyone who had been out all summer

along sea coasts and inland among strangers,
to the narratives, precisely recollected,
    that united them with all Tikigaq people.
Now the past returned. It *came round* to the present
    in the *things that had been said,* their genealogies and actions,
drawing lines from *back then* closer, so the kin ties
    between namesakes and their forebears reached the present
        unbroken.

All Tikigaq stories lay in two distinct strata, distinguished from each other by both time and content. Close to *now,* like the bones that lay in nuna, were the chronicles of recent forebears. These were true. They were histories: *the things that were said of them:* lives of ancestors, their names and genealogies, worked into each narrative.

Then there were the myths and legends, and archaic shaman sagas. These came from back-then: *taimmani*; no less true, the old men said, but because of their remoteness and their shamanistic content, separate.

As though to invoke the forebears' presence, *invite them* to the qalgi, the old men opened with the stories of the recent generations: great-great -grandparents' histories and people who came after. As they remembered, so they told them. They said:

Which families lived and struggled in those ruined iglus,
    which men set up the jaw-bones of each qalgi.
They told how *that* family of five brothers lived together
    in connected iglus at the west end of Tikigaq,
how their aana was a woman hunter:
    she killed seals like a man and sewed their noses to her parka.
How these brothers feuded with their neighbours,
    killed too many people and were exiled from the village:
while two younger men, whose partnership went out of balance,
    pulled back from their quarrel and ate meat together.

'This was where the shaman Suuyuk built his iglu.
    He was murdered at Uivvaq.
He had tried to keep the whales from Tikigaq.'
    'Kiasik, the wrestler, fought a stranger on the floorboards of
        this qalgi.'

'That was the summer Pauluagana shot a large bull caribou,
    and was cutting out the arrow, when he met a Siberian,

right there on Qipaluaq. The man tried to kill him.
You can still see the grave that Pauluagana dug him.'

'Kakianaq's wife. She was Pauluagana's daughter.
She became a shaman when the singing people took her.
They invited her. She went up there, beyond Qunusiq hill.
She returned in the autumn. She spoke a new language.
Kamik was her daughter. She understood her mother's language.'
'The madness of Aluuraq. It all started on the north side.
His brother snared a duck and Kinaviiraq claimed it.'

There were narratives, too, that illustrated ways
to judge the movement of the ice and currents,
how to predict the wind's direction,
which way to jump and turn the body and deploy equipment:
the measurement of force, slope, shift and counter-movement,
how to read the snow, clouds, winter lights and constellations.
And then stories of the great umialiks and the whales they'd taken.
How qalgi games and quarrels over whale shares turned to fighting.
About skinboats swept out by the ice and stranded,
how lost crews lived with people who wore walrus skins and
starved them.
About landfalls among strangers on *the other side,*
who spoke slowly and ate birds and animals large-boned and
sour-tasting.
Stories of how warriors came north and killed,
and how parties of men went south from here and took their women.

Of trading partnerships with inland people.
How boats set out with whale meat, seal oil and belukha,
returning with fawnskins, dried fish, beads and copper.
Of shamans who fought rivals from the high northern rivers,
dismembered their bodies and put them back together,
chasing off the animals their rivals hunted,
flew as wind through their qalgis and fire round their caches,
clashing with their souls on the moon and sea-bed.
All these were histories.

Next came stories from distant, remote winters,
in the time before *this* time, when the world was unfinished.
'When coasts were soft, and earth unstable.

It was night with no moon, and days without sunlight.
Snow was seal oil, seal oil was caribou.
   People walked on their hands on the hill-tops where the rocks
            had hardened,
and hunted the animals they heard barking in the darkness.

And people then were animals. Animals were people.
   They wore each other's masks and parkas.
The Raven man was man and raven. There were caribou people,
   ptarmigan and brown-bear women the first shamans married.
And the animals danced.
   Owl invited lemming, fox visited the wolverine,
wolves and squirrels had their qalgis,
   and all these *people* danced, and pushed their masks back,
showed their human faces in the fur-ruff's centre, and the shift of
            feathers.

And *people* exchanged gifts and spouses with their animal partners,
   held games in the qalgi with their cousins and brothers:
and men fought their wives on the iglu floor,
   were torn apart and eaten,
returned to life and died again, and took other women
   who were shamans and ate them.
And back then, everything on earth's crust had a song and was song.
   Rocks, bone, driftwood, excrement and water.
And song was soul thing, soul was its being.
   And all things, having soul, were alive with their song,
and singing, spoke their being, as the soul and song were.

And animals and people-who-were-animals
   in back time were magical and died only to come back again.
They weren't the real people who came later,
   who know death and hunger,
and must learn through their shamans
   who dreamed into back time,
and taught them the rituals the animals exact of them.

Yugaq: The Amulet Dances

The games led into a series of dances that continued at intervals through the autumn.

The dances were accompanied by whale-lung membrane drums whose circular wooden frames were struck from below. The sharp beat of the stick was thus harmonically enveloped in the deeper resonance of vibrating drum skins. Above the two-beat of percussion the drummers sang in a high register of syncopated half-tone phrases.

There were songs for all occasions, which the magical nature of words and melody made potent. Ritual songs were powerful both on account of the hypnotic vibrational impact of repeated exclamation and also for their origins.

Many songs had supernatural origin: they were learned in trance from spirits or animals, composed in dreams, inherited from forebears, transmitted by shamans who had realised them in ancient or strange languages.

Once a song was known and ingested it became part of the body. Sometimes the recipient took saliva from the singer's mouth to ensure the transfer of linguistic reality. The older a song, the more powerful its shamanistic life. But all these songs had spiritual validity provided they were performed word- and note-perfect in the right context. A song which was used where it had no place or ritual function was drained of virtue.

Many songs were also carefully and consciously composed to celebrate life events, conflicts, animals and places. These could be magical too, and become over time part of qalgi repertoire.

And just as songs were usually allusive and cryptic, often deliberately archaic or arcane in diction – sometimes a mere aya-ya-ya refrain set to a melodic line, or a scatter of fragmented ambiguities whose narrative sense was too well known to require explanation – so many dances traced familiar lore in abstract, compressed choreography.

Everyone had an inherited dance, and most people knew the songs that went with them. When a man took the qalgi floor, wearing his mittens with their clinking fawn's-hoof slices to help summon or appease the spirits, the drummers automatically, but with tentative and slightly absent strokes, inducted the rhythm of the dance he called for.

As the singers started the dancer swayed, stirred vaguely, described a few loose circles with his arms and gazed in front of him. Then the tempo gradually increased, the volume rose and the dancer, as though reluctant, ill at ease, perhaps even slightly bored, engaged a little further, though still sketching his movements to eliminate himself as far as possible from the dance pattern he had inherited or invented.

Ceremonial House Games

While the ancient stories rehearsed myth time, the games acted out in
silent diagram the conflicts in the story symbols: Raven and the uiluaqtaq
woman, moon brother/sun sister, light against darkness, hunter and ani-
mal, the forms of the games evoking the archaic fables in which animals
— quarrelsome, competitive and metamorphic — tricked one another,
fought, or mated, registered their evolution, confirmed their endurance.

    For animals, too, have their feast times and qalgis:
        each kind bound in name form to its company of spirits:
    societies of 'people', living underground, on land, or in the water,
        migrants, at death, moving south to where they've come from,
    again to take bodies, re enter the cycle.

    But whether souls range free, or wear animal meat and outer parkas,
        they sing, race, jump, dance, wrestle, and hold contests,
    inviting fellow species to their ceremonial houses,
        to contrive, where they can, both a welcome and a trouncing.

    In the stress and play of qalgi violence —
        tactics abstracted from their paths of impact,
    one story-creature on another —
        the lines of energy were rough and primal:

    as though birth-death, tangled in the players' bodies,
        rapped out the percussion — hunting, conflict, sexuality —
    most encounters between beings constitute.

    Likewise the winner-loser, host-guest oscillation,
        responsive and in counterpoint between the qalgis,
    maintained balance in their conflicts:
        the stress regulated to maintain an equilibrium,
    so winners who won were winners entirely,
        while the losers, when they lost, sprang back to become winners.

    Thus the games extended across Tikigaq in flexible symmetry,
        like the string figures children and old people wove,
    whose mobile patterns likewise enacted animal stories:
        foxes bounding through loops of seal thong,
    ptarmigan snared in complex thickets, caribou constructed
        out of geometric tangles, to collapse in the hands
    as the seal string resolved to the matrix of its circle.

But the point soon arrived where song and drum reached an intensity that the performer must follow. This, in other rituals, was the path the shaman entered, dancing to exhaustion till he 'died', allowing one of the souls inhabiting all humans to depart and range the mythic cosmos. The shaman lay in trance, sometimes bound with rope in foetal posture, until the freed soul returned from its mystical journey.

'Whereas shamanistic dancing had this special, extreme purpose, the qalgi dance was part of communal activity and the performance must unfold until its pattern was completed.

The form of the dance extended beyond the particularities of movement to a network of social and metaphysical connections: between dancer and audience, between kinsmen and namesakes who danced to each other, between host and guest qalgis, and between the living who danced and the ancestors whose gestures were enacted.

The first autumn dances also conjured the animals. Everyone was connected with one or more animals through amulets given at birth by a spiritual guardian from another qalgi.

According to the guardian's choice people carried wolf's teeth, foxtails, owl-, ptarmigan- and squirrel-skins, effigies of whales and walrus, eagles' heads and ravenskins. They wore these constantly: hanging them on cords round their necks, or on belts, in bags, or sewn to the outside of their parkas.

When they were sick people chewed their amulets to activate them with saliva, rubbed the amulet on birth- or death-stuff to generate still further power, used the amulet to massage their bodies and called on the animal spirit to help them.

The shaman's connections were still more intimate. He had visited the spirit homes of certain animals, or slept with an amulet bride in a dream and been torn up and eaten. Or he had learned seal, caribou or polar-bear language, or seen an animal reveal the human face of its inua that lay beneath the mask of its species.

The shaman carried amulets of animals which had taught him their lore in these visions. And when he was called on to perform in the qalgi, he could choose to transform to this amulet familiar.

> Then he'd slip
> into his other self and vanish through the katak:
> bear claws, loon's bill or wolftail flashing
> to confound the audience and signify his metamorphosis.

After the games the losers visited the winners' qalgi. They came up through the entrance-hole bearing spits full of meat held aloft and bundles of sinew and sealskin boot soles as gifts for the old people.

> Setting the meat in the middle of the qalgi,
>> they cried, 'We'll return!'
> The hosts reached for their meat, and answered with a roar as the
>> visitors withdrew.

Later that day, painted, in new skins, in half-masks, they returned with
their families. With gifts for namesakes, kinsfolk and guardians, they
came up in twos. When the qalgi was full they climbed up on to the roof
and looked down through the skylight.

> The visitors came dressed as their amulet animals.
>> They came to dance in amulet costumes:
> bear's nose and a loon's head –
>> polar bears and loons are both good divers,
> their amulets work well together –
>> wolf-head, wolfskin ruff and wolftail,
> wolverine, jaws open and claws hanging,
>> half one skin, half another, half snowy owl, half squirrel,

> half fur outside, half turned-out leather,
>> half black and ochre faces,
> half the face bare to signify the double amulet,
>> dancing for their guardians and namesakes.

> And the dancers cry in their amulet voices,
>> in the voices of their helping animals:
> brown bear, red fox, peregrine and golden eagle,
>> raven, gull and marmot, grebe and lemming,
> double being, dancing to their doubles,
>> song and drum beat, shouting through the katak,
>>> 'Ui! Ui!
> Ui! Ui!,

> dancing to their living namesakes,
>> the dead namesakes' dances:
> through the animals and souls
>> they killed and worshipped.

Since the tempo of song has quickened, the dancer's movements grow more muscular and sharply angled. The calm of the first patterns, the vague eyes and drifting feet, transform to a rhythmically percussive flood of gestures, diagraming stories, lives and visions.

The hands harpoon, the arms paddle kayaks,
    the dancer hunts, he triumphs, opening his chest, lets fly with arrows.
Stamping with the drums, the right foot shakes the qalgi
    and the high arms cross, the open hands
flex, curve, invite, control, placate, defend, invoke,
    conjure the dance signs that the maker jointed.

Whether it is character that flows
    through the weaving-without-person
that the dancer created with his first design,
    or the force of dance-form
that drives hands, voice, arms and feet,
    it's uncertain who is dancing there:
man, spirit, ancestor or some compound of these,
    while from the dancer's centre the amulets fly outwards,
tails, beaks, teeth and feathers flung and shaking,
    till the spirits approach and the dance is spirit.

The dancer is a loon, he juts his neck, retracts, recoils,
    his hard eye flicks, and his half-open mouth,
unhuman with dance cry, reveals his own shadow
    and the spirit of the teaching animal.

As the souls in the dance-joints loosen and stream free,
    the bird's-neck rhythm of his nodding from a straight trunk
jerks the chin through regulated spasms;
    hands and feathers mask and unmask,
and the dancer's face disc, opening to show its forebears,
    merges and dissolves with them.

'That dance was *him*!'
    The elders who have seen the forebears know its antecedent.
Woven into compound being
    and played on a screen
the drum has stretched across the present,
    the song ends abruptly and the dancer pauses.
Poised on one foot, he balances in silence,
    till the next masked dancer leaps up through the katak.

3. Spring: The Whale Hunt

This narrative poem concluded the book and contains a new kind of writing. Based partly on experience of the whale hunt and uqaluktuaq (ancestor histories), this poem contains a fictionalised story, a new uqaluktuaq which is infused with some of the folkloric ideas introduced earlier in the book. One mystifying ambiguity lies in the character of the young shaman – a version of the 'poor boy' described in the Summer initiation passages. Fraudulent shamans unmasked by boys make frequent appearances in old stories. Whether this young man is himself a charlatan, a hysteric or a visionary struggling to control his insight remains unspoken.

When the sun came up on the hill called Vertebra and the snow birds were nesting in the village, Asatchaq sang this for the skinboat, which was down from its rack and standing by the qalgi:

> *Paammaguuq pamma*
> *aanalukpin!*
> *Iqigiin! Iqigiin!*

> Up there, up there!
> Aana's going to beat you!
> Wake up!
> Wake up skinboat!

> *Samaruna*:
> The boat has slept all winter.
> An old woman will wake it.
> It will fly, it will swim
> when they take it on the water.

> *Asatchaq*:
> At 'Covering Boats' moon,
> when a north wind blows,
> the men build a snow-house by their qalgi.
> Here they'll wrap their boat-frames,
> with last spring's sealskins.

The dehaired skins have been soaked under sea-ice. The qalgi women sew them into one and cut rope-holds round the edges. When the gunwhales have been oiled the men spread the skin and lash it to the boat-frame's horizontals. It dries taut and supple.

Samaruna:
It will fly like a sea-bird.
The skin and skeleton
are light and flexible.
They can never be broken.

Outside each snow-house the umialiks feed the village children.

Asatchaq:
The whales are generous.
Hunters must be generous.
If umialiks share meat
with children and old people,
the whales will approach them.

Samaruna:
Then they call for a child,
and they call an old woman.
'Take this sack.
Go down to *nali!*'

The child walks to the south beach (nali). There he gathers sticks. The men prop the skinboat on its paddles. When the child returns the men build a fire beneath the boat prow.

Asatchaq:
The men light the fire.
The woman approaches.
She stands at the prow.
She sings for the skinboat.

Samaruna:
This makes it fast
and makes it quiet.
The prow has been warmed.
It won't stick to the ice
when the hunters launch it.

The day before they go out on the sea-ice the umialiks wake early and the wife walks to the skinboat.

The woman is wearing wolftail mittens. She sweeps out the boat with her left-hand mitten. Then she lifts her waterpot and pours water on the gunwhales.

Then they load the boat with their equipment. Harpoons, lances, spears and cutting tools are strapped to the bottom.

They load lines and drag-floats, grapples, hooks, harpoon blades. The harpooner carries his ivory harpoon rest.

The umialik's amulets are hung from the boat ribs. He has kept the shavings from his shafts and paddles. He takes these with him.

On the morning they go out, the woman calls her crew and feeds them.

Asatchaq:
The men must eat.
The umialiks eat nothing.

Samaruna:
The channel is open.
The spirits have caught a whale already!

Asatchaq:
It is time to go hunting.
The shamans have told them
the spirits' instructions.
The look-out men run home from the sea-ice:

Samaruna:
'Puiyaqpulguuq!
Puiyagpulguuq!
The first whales are spouting!
Belukhas are running!'

The men harness themselves to their boat-sled. They are ready to go hunting.

But they wait for the woman. She walks ahead of them. As the men start to pull, the side of the skinboat brushes her parka.

She runs across the men's path. She lets the far side of the skinboat brush her.

The woman leads the skinboat to the south shore. Where the beach meets the ice, again she stops to let it touch her.

Once they've come to the sea-ice the woman falls behind the boat-sled. The husband follows her, always singing. The amulets sewn to their parkas tremble.

The autumn before, during the qalgi rituals, each couple had walked to the Point to look for a crayfish that the waves had stranded." They built a little ice-house and laid the crayfish inside with its head pointing inland. Then they gave it fresh water.

Now, as the crew drags the boat-sled to the sea-ice, they visit their umialik's crayfish iglu.

The husband takes his harpoon and cuts round the ice-house. When they lift the roof off, there's the crayfish!

Ah! Everyone laughs!
 The woman rolls the crayfish, belly up.
They laugh again.
 It's like a whale.
The skeleton! The skeleton!
 The same thing will happen.
They'll roll the whale over!

The woman lifts the crayfish. She uses her left hand. She carries her pot in her right-hand mitten. When they reach open water the husband takes a thread of baleen, ties the crayfish to a stone and sinks it.

The woman drops her right-hand mitten in the skinboat. It will stay in the boat until the hunt is over. She passes each man her ritual pot. They all drink water.

They have come to the ice-coast through a defile full of pot-holes in a sheltering pressure ridge.

Vast plains of ice-rocks he behind them. The snow by the channel is fresh and untrodden. Ahead, the sea opens. Tikigaq has vanished.

Secluded from their rivals, the umialiks choose a small bay in the ice-rim. Here they will wait for whales to approach them.

Now they have come the crew is silent. The wife and husband gesture their instructions. The men unload. They slide the skinboat to the ice-rim. The harpoon juts across the water. When the floats have been rigged to the drag-line, and the drag-line has been coiled, the harpooner climbs in to his front bench. The crew take their places in twos behind him. The umialik follows. They move off slowly. Ice-floes drift past. They pretend to go hunting. Alone by the boat-sled, the woman takes her belt off. Still holding her pot, she lies on the ice with her head pointing inland. She waits for the harpooner. When the men have travelled out some way, they turn the boat and paddle back again. They reach the ice-edge; the harpooner rises.

Samaruna:
The harpooner leans out with his weapon.
The harpooner harpoons her.
He touches her neck
through the hood of her parka.

Asatchaq:
The woman stands up.
She faces inland.
She starts to walk home.

Samaruna:
She doesn't look back.
She leaves her belt.
She leaves her mitten.

Asatchaq:
She walks home to Tikigaq.
When she reaches the qalgi,
She goes to the rack
where the boat lay all winter.

She unlashes the planks and carries them home where she leans them
against the iglu passage.

Then she enters the iglu. She hangs her pot above the katak. She lays
her mitten by the oil lamp.

Samaruna:
Her husband wears the belt
his wife has left him.
Her right-hand mitten
lies in the skinboat.

Asatchaq:
The wife has not eaten.
Now someone cuts meat for her.
If she cut meat herself,
she would break the harpoon line.

The woman does nothing to frighten the whale or put the boat in
danger.

Samaruna:
She does not sew or comb her hair.
She speaks quietly and moves slowly.
She pretends to be sick.
She sits and does nothing.

The sun moves round the hills and over the peninsula. It sets on the western ice-horizon. The men stand all night in their double parkas. Inside their mittens they wear fawnskin gloves. Their boots are lined with bird's-down and shavings.

Samaruna:
They've thrown their winter clothes out.
They wear new clothes for the whale hunt.

Asatchaq:
The oil and blood on their winter skins
made their old clothes disgusting.

Out of the village the snow is untrodden. The ice is clean. The sea is empty.

The men watch and do nothing. They eat raw meat; they drink cold water.

When they finish their meat the crew's 'little muskrat' runs to the village. The muskrat boy is too young to go whaling. He's quick; he's strong. He runs between village and the sea-ice. The hunters need meat. The woman umialik fills the little muskrat's bucket. The boy runs back with it.

The men take their knives. They eat a little. Briefly, in turns, they sleep on the boat-sled.

Asatchaq:
In the winter we slept.
If we slept now on the sea-ice
the whales would pass us.
We would never see them.

The men wait. They do nothing. They watch the light, they watch the sea. They scan the clouds and the horizon.

Crowds of duck and belukha go through. The men fish for crabs with grids made of baleen. The old men recite the Raven Man's story.

Samaruna:
Raven killed the first whale.
The men tell his story
to make whales come to Tikigaq.

Asatchaq:
And they tell the story of Aninatchaq.
Aninatchaq knew when the whales were coming.
He told his umialik:

'When the sun touches *Vertebra*
a whale will come up by your skinboat.
You will harpoon it.'

Samaruna:
While his men fished for crabs,
and the sun touched Vertebra,
this is what happened.

Asatchaq:
And my grandfather Suuyuk gave me this song.
It *swept the whales to him:*

Sumun makua tililagich
agvitvichli tililagich
uvuna imma Tikigagmun.

Where shall I tell
the whales to go?
 I want to sweep them into Tikigaq!

Samaruna said:
These small whales, inutuqs,
small round fat ones
come to us from down there,
 from their country south of us.

Asatchaq:
The women sit at home.
They are whale souls in their iglus.
The whales listen and sing.
They hear Tikigaq singing.

Samaruna:
Listen to the north wind!
Listen to the sea-ice!
Listen to the inutuq
rising, breathing!

The boatskin drums, and the swell climbs the ice-rim.
   An inutuq rises. Warm steam drifts across the crewmen's faces.
Aapaah! breathing! *Aapaah!* breathing!

      The harpooner stands. He raises his weapon.
The whale hangs by the skinboat stern.
      Alone in the bow, the harpooner waits to be manoeuvred.
The crewmen freeze.
      The inutuq's back fills the slits in their goggles.
Squatting at the rim, the umialik leans forward
      and works the boat round with a hand and paddle.
As the prow swings in the current tilts it.
      The harpooner stumbles. He trips on the drag-floats.
His elbow strikes the gunwhale. He staggers up again and lunges.
      The inutuq dives. The blade stutters and bounces.
The harpooner falls backward. His shaft drops in the water.
      The skinboat pitches.
The crew extend pole hooks, spears and grapples.
      The harpooner grabs a paddle and retrieves his weapon.
He turns the boat and sculls back to ice-camp.

Asatchaq:
The children will laugh.
The women will scold him:
'He didn't brace his back leg!'
'The harpooner fell over!'
'He could have struck that inutuq!'
'He should have waited!'

In ecstasy once, the harpooner Kunannauraq,
      woken from his trance of concentration
– eight shamans in one skinboat luring the whale to them –
      hurled his weapon vertically
above the whale that had risen by his skinboat
      – as though Tikigaq itself rose! –

and the harpoon turned, blade downward, diving like a sea-bird,
    planted in its death-place, deep between the vertebrae.

The north wind drops and the channel closes. The men stow their
equipment and drag their boats back.

Samaruna:
Maybe a *south wind* shaman has been singing.'
Perhaps someone has tied the ice together.

Asatchaq:
It was the shaman Uqpik who did that.
He fitted four sticks
to the sides of an ice-crack.

Samaruna:
He tied two sticks with men's hair,
and two sticks with women's.

Asatchaq:
That was how Uqpik closed the channel.

Samaruna:
When shamans get angry,
they can stop whales coming.

Asatchaq:
That's what my grandfather Suuyuk did.
He was angry with the people.
He tried to starve Tikigaq.
The umialiks killed him.

The umialiks send for a *north wind* shaman:
    a shaman who loves hunting, and wants to see animals.
The shaman brings his drum and an assistant.
    They sit, and he drums. His soul goes out.
He travels to the sea-bed.
    Some woman lives down there. She has food. She keeps animals.
Maybe she'll help them when the shaman has visited.
    Or he goes to the house of the north wind spirit.
He tells the wind's inua:
    'The people are hungry! Tikigaq needs whale meat!'

The wind turns round. The pack-ice retreats.
  They paddle to fresh inlets where the lane is narrow.
Snow settles, clinks, blows on and off the sleeves of their parkas.
  A fog moves in. It is white. There is nothing.
Ducks land in the silence. Blind, they listen.
  'Listen!' Nothing. And then, 'Listen.' Harsh, long breathing.
The harpooner's right hand grips his weapon.
  A whale has breached. An inutuq is breathing.
The men slide the boat from the green, smooth edge
    the young *little muskrat* has cleared with his scraper

          otherwise your aana's
          going to beat you.

Sunk to its handle, the helmsman's long blade stirs the current.
  They labour. They travel. Mush clouds in the water thicken.
The pack is moving. Their wake tumbles between ice-blocks.
  The inutuq breaches. 'Ahead. There. By the mush-ice!'
The water heaps, then plunges the skinboat back and downward.
  Up-current, the whale emerges and rolls.
The men on the far side drive their blades through the torrent,
  the near three men, where the inutuq can hear them,
flatten their paddles to the skinboat's belly.

As the whale breathes out, they slacken their paddles.
  The skin shuffles and drags. The beak grinds into ice-mush.
'Young ice!' *Aana's going to beat you!*
  The men back-paddle. The harpooner reaches forward.
He cuts round the prow with the blade of his weapon.
  Ahead, the whale escapes under water. It swims underneath.
The young ice buckles. The skinboat is stranded.

          A bag of young wolf-skulls,
              a bird's head and a dog's.
          Five red pebbles, and two molluscs
              his grandfather found in a stomach.

          The umialik shakes
              the sealskin container.
          Its ornaments rattle.
              The amulets jump.

He whispers to their spirits:
It is now and it was then.
The animals came.
And now you are coming.
Right here to us!
Come here to us!

Under a small board fitted to the prow in front of the harpooner,
    hangs a whale in half-relief, its flippers spread,
tail flush with the board's edge. Modelled from above,
    as if viewed rising through the current, the whale hangs,
unseen, upside-down, back flooded with the grain of water:
    eyes, dark blue trade-beads, pinned blind to each side
of a head traced with one sweep of the carver's burin.
    As though summoning the whale through the plank at his knee,
the harpooner taps sharply on its angled surface.

'*Puigin agviq!*
Puigin agviq!'

Rise whale!
Rise whale!

The fog lifts in the silence. The whale has vanished.

There is waiting. Or there's going round or forcing a way through.
    There is singing to disperse the ice,
and there's watching for a lane to open.
    Drifting across the skinboat's stern,
the white, older ice moves in and sweeps the mush round them.
    The sun climbs. Ducks and guillemots fly rapidly over.
The crewmen rest. It is warm.
    They are locked in their pond of open water.
Their faces are seamed, as they watch the surface,
    by stitches in the boat's reflection.

The umialik gazes round. He laughs.
    His voice climbs steeply, then slants quickly down.
'Maybe since the young ice holds us / we'll wait for the time being.'
    A clatter of birds reinforces the silence.

They wait in silence, and the wind is silent.
 Then: 'Who has a song?' the umialik ponders.
The mush-ice presses the boatskin through its framework.
 'My song or your father's?' answers a young shaman.
The nose of his mask is a vertical, forked whale's tail,
 raised eyebrows, in the gesture of a *Yes,* are branching whale flukes.
'Put on your mask then,' the umialik mutters.
 The shaman's face spins.
The mask-holes eat his eyes and cheekbones.
 The harpooner turns away. 'We need that man's paddle.
I'll kill him if he stays out shamanising.
 Kinnaq una! Fool!' he whispers. 'Your family is hungry.'
Then, 'Come back!' he shouts, and lifts his weapon.
 The flukes on the whale-mask slap and go under.
'*Yai!*' from the stern, the umialik counters.
 'All right!' he agrees. 'Seven paddles might do it.'

The young shaman is still raving.
 The man behind him tears a mitten from his shaman nephew,
and plugs the splashing mouth with dogskin.
 '*Kitaa!* Come on!' The umialik stabs at the slush with his paddle.
The harpooner jumps forward.
 He cuts a triangular section below him.
The men slice down and back with their paddles.
 The boat edges forward.
'*Alla suli!* And another! *Alla suli!*'
 'Like an eight-flippered ugruk!'
'But,' smiling at the shaman, 'one flipper's missing!'
 'That's the shaman asleep in the ugruk's belly!'

When they reach hard white ice, they drag the boat up.
 The slush drains and they clean their paddles.
The young men take their parkas off and rub snow on their bodies.
 The older men sleep. They all drink from their pouches.
They've lost the boat-sled. There is nothing to eat.
 'And our bucket of food!' The umialik laughs.
The shaman sings out: '*Arii!* I'm hungry!'
 'We thought something ate you!' says his uncle.

The harpooner broods at the skinboat prow.
 The parchment is scarred, but the stitches and the lashing hold.

Just some of his equipment is disrupted.
     The broad, thin, slate harpoon blade, with its owner's mark –
in five rhythmical cuts, a quadrangular caribou,
     tail lifted, two legs visible – has snapped across the middle.
'The nest . . . the nest . . .' the umialik whispers.
     Wedged in the boat-frame lies his harpoon blade-box:
egg-shaped, the lid studded with a crystal,
     and bound into place with braided sinew.
The harpooner extracts a fresh slate from the set of five,
     and tamps down the shavings that pack the remainder.

'Your harpoon rest,' the umialik gestures.
     'I know,' he grunts.
'You knocked it. When you fell. The thongs are loose.'
     'I'll tie them.'
His left hand raises the two polar bears' heads
     carved on the shanks of the ivory harpoon rest.
Their eyes are inlaid. Their teeth are serrated.
     'Your left-handed partner!' he jokes with the umialik.
The white ruff with its bear's snout screens the helmsman's laughter.
     Two eagles engraved on the stock of the harpoon rest
rear off the boat floor. Their feathers dangle.
     Each grasps a whale in extended talons.

It is brilliant and windy. Cumulus banked on the white horizon
     blows south against the movement of the ice-pack.
They coast with the floe drift, then paddle up-current.
     We're the last of the whale camps. The first run is over.
The umialik scans his men's new fawnskin parka backs.
     Their long hoods dangle. The wolf ruffs shine.
Everything's too late! too clean!
     Someone must have struck a whale already.
Each of his boot-legs shows a bleached skin panel.
     Even a young man can have three, or even five of those.
Some older umialiks have caught so many –
     a panel for each whale they've taken –
their whole boot-top is bleached sealskin panels.

Still. Yes. Two springs back, when I caught an inutuq,
     all the umialiks raced to claim their own portions.
It was an inutuq, a big inutuvak.

Who got the first share? It was Aquppak.
(His soul once travelled to the country of the whales.)
   Aquppak's boat lay nearest, and he heard my signal.
All down coast the umialiks followed,
   singing and waving their spears and paddles.
My inutuq dived; it escaped below the shore-fast ice.
   It came up to breathe and we chased the drag-float.
There was oil in the wake. We followed the colour.
   We travelled all night. Then Aquppak passed us.
His harpooner killed it. With one hit, they told me.
   After I'd taken the tail and flippers, and my crew had their portion,
Aquppak won the first share of my inutuq.
(When he'd carried his meat home, he tried to send the ice out.
   We almost lost everything. Aquppak's a shaman.)
Next came Niguvana and his crew. They had lost their harpoon.
   All they had were knives and lances. But they knew how to use them.
Who came third? Qipugaluatchiaq? His first wife was a caribou.
   He turned into a polar bear one winter.
Fourth. It was Piquk. Then came Kakianaq. He died last summer.
   He ate the wrong meat — a pregnant woman gave it to him.
Last came Aqsaqauraq (no one can touch him with a knife or arrow),
   Mammaninna, Isigraqtuaq and cross-eyed Ipiq.
Pauluagana, Nigliq and Nannuna also came: but they got nothing.
   Then old man Aulagruaq arrived. He had only three crewmen.
All the shares had been taken already.
   Who else had a boat? It was Kamik: his first season.
Kamik took a share of Piquk's whale. But he gave it away.
   He carried the meat round and gave it to old people.
Perhaps he'll get a whale next season.

Yes. Six whales were taken.
   The boats from one qalgi didn't get a whale.
That qalgi was Suagvik.
   Their boats got shares from the all others.
Qagmaqtuuq got two whales last season.
   It's said that Suagvik took eleven whales one spring.
None of the other houses got one whale between them.

They have come to a place lying west of the peninsula.
   'Down coast! Down wind!' the umialik gestures.
The young shaman drags his blade and then sculls briskly.

The marks on their paddles have eroded.
'No whale . . . no belukha. The sea is empty.'
They paddle and then drift. They zig-zag south again.
Then: '*Avataqpak*: Drag-float!' the harpooner whispers.
They hang their paddles and watch the sealskin ride towards them.
The young shaman picks his ear with a finger.
His whale-mask is contorted.
'Listen to the float-mask! Listen to it singing!'
The harpooner encloses a smile in his mitten.
The men fold their paddles to the skinboat's belly.
The float bounds closer. It is dark against the water.
First one song, then a second *aya-ya-ya*,
    cross-syncopated from the distance, cross the sea-ice.
'Maybe your cousin Tikiq is a mask-float?'

The harpooner turns to the shaman's uncle.
    'That's Tikiq. And now Aquppak, singing across there.'
The umialik tugs an ear and gestures silence.
    The men grip their paddles.
The sealskin scuttles and comes up again.
    The swollen flippers claw the surface.
A big inutuq emerges. It breathes noisily and slow.
    The float-mask with its downturned mouth rolls nearer.
'My cousin Mitik was raped by a float-mask,' the young shaman stammers.
    'Her child was born crazy.' The umialik starts counting.
When I've come to twice fifteen, the whale will rise here.

        Puigin aqviq! Pui gin agviq!
        Rise whale! Rise whale!

If the whale's not badly wounded, the float may pull the blade out.
    '*Ki!*' he whispers. The skinboat shoots forward.
The drag-float crashes across their gunwhales.
    Beneath them the water is full and solid.
Ii! Yes! Old man Tikiq's!
    The float-mask rears. Its mouth is rigid.
I was there in the qalgi when he carved that face disc.
    He brought jade from Kobuk for its eyes and lip plugs.
The boat keel rides the whale's back.
    The whale hangs from their paddles.
The men feel it bursting against their boot soles.

70

Anaugaa! He hits it. The harpooner strikes downward.
   The blade slits the skin and passes through the blubber.
The hunter twists the hand shaft, and the blade uncouples.
   The broad thin slate reaches down through the muscle.
The foreshaft roots in the clinging blubber.
   The blade runs sideways. It slants along the tissue.
The hand shaft falls across the front two benches.

As the shaft rolls away, the harpooner sings.
   The line must run smooth.
The float must drag the whale back. It must drag it to the surface.
   The harpooner sings downward. Then he spits in the water.
As the line travels out, the song moves with it.
   The hunter spits to make the song go further, travel faster.
That's how I learned it. My uncle taught me. The song went to my mind.
   He put saliva on his finger and I ate it.
That's how I've kept the song he carried.

Quickly the umialik, holding the boat rigid
   with his hand on the paddle, unlashes his boot thongs.
Nothing must be tight and knotted. Otherwise the line will tangle.
   The line rushes out, and the floats jump free.
They fly across the gunwhale and hit the water.

The whale rises, and the drag-floats hold it.
   Two harpoon lines stream from the neck skin.
The skinboat pivots. The stern swings across the tail.
   Three men work their paddles.
Three others grab their knives and lances.
   They have long flint pole-knives. They have spears and lances.
Two men stab the whale's cheek.
   'Tail!' shouts the umialik.
'Attack the throat!' the harpooner whispers.
   The whale starts to roll. The stern pitches as the tail emerges.
'Cut the sinew!' The umialik punches.
   With a boot on the whale he slashes down and into the tendons.
A man follows with a knife and, staggering across,
   his bench-partner swings his own blade in and sideways.
The tail arches and the flukes slump in the water.
   'Three now! Four spears!'
The head re-emerges. The mouth rotates upward.

71

The men fight past each other to the forward gunwhale.
They open the throat. They run the breast through.
    'Blood . . .' mutters the young shaman. He sits freezing in the middle.
Half out of water, the whale's eye follows the umialik.
    The harpooner chops at the outlet in the whale's breast.
It is sunset. It is many rivers.
    On the convex of the whale's eye, the young shaman sees his
        mask inverted.

It's still breathing! (the umialik).
    'It's trying to breathe. It's still alive!'
The mouth closes, then drops open. Baleen rattles.
    Oil, blood and mucus froth in the blowholes.
It slides along the whale's cheek.
    '*Arii!* it's weeping!'
A plume of blood and water forks across the skinboat.
    There is no inhalation.
                The singing comes closer.

Tikiq's skinboat appears in the distance.
    We could have eaten that first wound, the umialik ponders.
We could have cut out his harpoon; destroyed the drag-float.
    They say Kamik did that once. Whose whale was it?
He cut out the first harpoon blade, and hid it in his parka sleeve.
    My grandfather told me . . . Yes. It was Suuyuk's. Suuyuk's . . .

But the blade left its owner's mark.
    Kamik kept seeing it.
When he cut into that whale, he saw the owner's mark in it.
    It was there on the skin, on the heart and liver.
He ate the mark. He died that summer.
    The owner's mark got him.

The bow-poles of Tikiq's skinboat lightly bump them.
    Tikiq sits at the stern.
He unhoods and breathes quietly.
    His lip-plugs are beads set in mastodon ivory.
He has thin grey whiskers.

The two crews grasp each other's gunwhales.
    The two groups gaze into the distance.
Gulls start arriving.

I've killed this whale. It's old man Tikiq's.
The birds must also have their portion.

Tikiq scans a cloud-bar on the ice horizon.
    'Thank you.' His voice stops.
He transfers his paddle.
    'My harpooner struck it. But not hard enough, maybe.
We lost it. Thank you.'

Tikiq bends down. He picks something up.
    It is white and oily.
Tikiq throws it. It lands on the whale's back.
    It's the tail of a belukha.
Some old umialiks do that. One day I shall ask him.

'Ii . . . Yes . . . Suluk!'
    The old man *names* the younger umialik.
He names him. He laughs softly.
    'We thought you were dead!
Maybe your wife has taken a new husband!'

'We were stranded in the young ice.
    There. On the north side.
It was my fault.
    Here is your whale.
We recognised your drag-float.'

'This must be the whale the Moon Spirit sent me.'
    Tikiq stands up. He is looking for a bag.
'You get the first share.
    Next year you'll catch your own whale.'
'Thank you.'

Tikiq bends. He digs in the stern.
    He stands up, holding the skin of a raven.
'We thought your crew had been swept off, and lost.'
    He steps out of his boat and displaces the harpooner.
'Someone has been murdered.'

Tikiq stands on the whale's head, taking his knife out.
    'It was someone from Katak's boat.'
His boots gleam in the bloody water.

He scratches a section, slices through the skin,
and plunges the raven's head into the blubber.
'Eat!' he murmurs. *That raven was hungry.*

Someone in Katak's boat has been murdered.

Tikiq withdraws the raven's beak.
It is hot and oily.
He opens the wings.
He throws one, then the other across his shoulders.
The head wags over the umialik's tonsure.
The bill scrapes his forehead.

Kaa! screams Raven Man.
Kaa! cries Raven.

Aquppak arrives. Niguvana's boat arrives. Ipiq follows.
The whale has turned over. It floats on its back.
Five skinboats surround it.
The men sit and talk quietly.
Tikiq plants a harpoon in the white-blazed chin.
He fixes a blade for towing the body.
'Just like my whiskers . . .'
Tikiq jerks the hairs between his chin and parka ruff.
'We'll follow,' says Suluk.

Each crew fixes a lance in the carcass. The umialiks plant spears in their
order of arrival. The five boats link tow ropes. They drag the dead whale
to the nearest sea-ice.

Ui! Ui!
Tikiq leads them.
Tikiq leads the joy cry.
Ui! Ui!
Suluk leads the umialiks that follow.

When they get to the ice, the men cut off the tail flukes. They strip
maktak from the throat and the five crews eat it. When three more
boats have come they cut skin and blubber from the stomach. Everyone
eats maktak.

Samaruna:
They use someone's foot.
They use the man with the longest foot
to measure their maktak.

Asatchaq:
Only the first eight boats get shares.
The others get something.
But they don't get shares.

They lower the flukes into the first umialik's boat. The men haul the boat to safe, flat ice. Here they'll butcher the carcass.

Samaruna:
They follow the songs
of the first umialik.
They sing as they travel.

When the eight crews get to the butchering site the whale's body is moored to the ice-rim and in turn each umialik with his long pole-knife marks the share he's entitled to.

First they mark the back and top sides. Then they roll the whale over and mark the belly. The first boats get the largest portions. It is divided as follows:

Anirruuk: the whole body from tail to navel. The first umialik takes it.

Avarrak: the two tail flukes belong to the first umialik.

Ini: a strip down the middle of the first umialik's share. It goes to the umialik's shaman.

Taliguk: the flippers are shared by umialiks and crews of the first and second boats.

Qimigluich: the back and sides, from blowholes to mid-tail, is taken by the first umialik's crewmen.

Silviich: the belly and sides surrounding the flippers. This is taken by the second and third boats.

Qaa and *Qaglu:* the lower left-hand jaw is taken by the fourth and fifth boats. The lower right-hand jaw belongs to the sixth and seventh boats.

Tapsinaaq: a strip, one footstep wide, round the whale behind the navel. The eighth boat gets this.

Niksiutaq: the top of the head – all skin and blubber – is shared by everyone. In this way the last boats get a portion.

Tirragiigraq: a triangle of maktak from the bottom jaw. Everyone eats it while they're butchering.

Internal pans: the heart, lungs, liver, tongue, intestines, kidneys, membrane, sinew, jaw-bones, baleen, ribs and vertebrae are taken by the first umialik.

Asatchaq:
This is how the whale is cut
when the first umialik,
over many seasons,
has taken more than five whales.

Samaruna:
But it's different
when the first umialik,
even over many seasons,
has killed fewer than five whales.

Asatchaq:
If he has had fewer than five,
he keeps the tail
and shares it in the autumn.

Samaruna;
Umialiks who've had more than five
share the tail
in late winter, before whaling.

'My wife will be expecting something.'
    Tikiq works a pole-knife through the water,
and his man hooks a portion of flipper to the surface.
    They step back on the ice.
The current swings the boat across the whale's side.
    'I shall send Nanmak. He's a fast runner.'

Tikiq cores the blubber and slots maktak on to a paddle blade.
    The runner extracts the wife's mitten from the skinboat.
He waits to be sent into Tikigaq, to Tikiq's iglu.

'Ii . . . Yes . . . Suluk . . .' The older man *names* Suluk.
    The name *Suluk* touches him.
His name gently strikes him.
    'Send for your wife too.'
The younger umialik looks abashed and down.
    All the women will come out on the ice now.
My wife will come with them.
    'Put maktak on your paddle. Send a runner.
Your wife and mine will greet the whale together.'
    He is putting me forward. Next winter I'll repay him.

'This is your whale. Your own wife will greet it.
    Your wife will bring the whale freshwater.
My wife will come with the rest of the women.'
    'Maybe, then, next spring, you'll get your own whale.'

'But since you are sending your messenger to Tikigaq,
    I too will send a runner. He will help bring our sleds out.'

The younger umialik returns to his skinboat.
    The men were hungry. They are resting.
The young shaman is slumped on the ice by the skinboat.
    He wakes and his mask rocks, front-down, by his shoulder.

'Ki! Run into Tikigaq. Bring our sleds out!'
    'Arii!' he cries. 'But I'm a shaman!'
'Get up. Hurry. How long will the ice wait? I can hear it creaking.
    The whale is hot. It will stink. We want fresh meat.
Its stomach is boiling. Get up. Hurry.'
    The umialik turns away. He speaks aloud.
'Perhaps there are other shamans in my skinboat.'
    The harpooner is fixing a blade to his weapon.
'Perhaps those other shamans don't say much.
    Perhaps you didn't understand them.'
There is laughter from beside the skinboat.
    The shaman hears, but he cannot see.
'Maybe they made this whale approach our skinboat.

Maybe it was they who brought our share of it.'

Up he staggers. He is weeping. 'Don't let your eyes freeze.'

'Don't stumble on your lip-plugs,' the harpooner shouts after him.
'I knew about it when you told me,'

the younger umialik gestures down-coast to the lower icecamps.
'I saw his brother from the distance.

There was blood on their boat. They were looking for someone.'

'You have sent the boy home. You have done well.

If he had stayed, there would have been fighting.

He is Katak's nephew.

I was there when it happened.

It was Katak's first whale.'

The older man's voice is flat and boneless.

'I shall tell what happened.

They were standing together. Nannuna and Katak.

They were standing in his skinboat.

Katak said: 'Ii . . . That's my share. But I'll give it away.'

That's what Katak said.

'So mine starts here.'

Nannuna said this. I was there. I heard it.

Maybe Nannuna's knife went too far along the middle.

They couldn't agree where to cut along the middle.

That's when they started. They wrestled in the skinboat.

Their men were on the ice. They held the skinboat.

But Nannuna was too old. Katak climbed on top of him.

Nannuna's head was over the benches.

He tried to get his knife out.

He would have killed Katak. But he couldn't find it.

Then Nannuna's brother jumped into the skinboat.'

The gathered umialiks uneasily listen.

Tikiq looks down and scrapes a foot. 'A hunter must be generous.

He must think of the people. They all have stomachs.

My crew's stomachs are no larger than the others . . .

'Yes: Nannuna's brother. He jumped in the skinboat.

But he couldn't do anything.

The boat started rolling. The two men fell over.

They were both in the water. Katak swam for the ice-edge.

But Nannuna's brother leaned out and grabbed him.

78

He grabbed him by the lashings.
Katak's boots were open.
He'd undone his lashings when he caught the whale.
He tried to reach the ice-edge.
He tried getting to his people.
But Nannuna's brother held his lashings.
He dragged him under by the lashings.'

It is hot on the ice.
The two men leave their parkas on the skinboat benches.
They run bare-chested.
Nanmak wears the umialik's mitten.
He carries the paddle across his shoulder.
Black skin and white blubber hood the paddle's markings.

Even if the shaman asks me, I shall say nothing.
I saw what happened.
I was there when Nannuna's brother murdered Katak.
Katak drowned quickly.
His brother pulled Nannuna from the water.
They escaped together. They left their skinboat.
They'll have tried to leave Tikigaq before anyone gets them.
(Katak's brother is a man who never misses.
Last winter he killed Ayuviina with a single arrow.)
I saw Katak's brother's crew approaching.
There'll be blood on that skinboat.

And this boy who runs beside me:
some people say he's a genuine shaman –
that he's visited the whaling spirits –
and flown to the moon's house – masked and unmasked –
talks the spirits' language. I don't know anything.
Others say he's lazy, crazy – he never goes hunting –
he pretends – he's a liar – ants to be a shaman.
They say he said this:
that he-was-his-own-mother's-mother-and-that-she-made-Raven,
and-that-he-was-the-whale-that-Raven-harpooned-when-
Raven-harpooned-Tikigaq.

I say nothing. He is Katak's nephew.
Why wasn't he in Katak's boat-crew?

Or his older cousin's? They say no one wanted him.
Then Suluk's boat took him.
He'll go mad when he hears his uncle has been murdered.

The two men follow the boat-sled's trail to Tikigaq.
There are ponds on the surface.
Snow melts from the ridges and their blue cores glow.
The two climb the south beach. There is grass and driftwood.
Nanmak grips the paddle in the woman's mitten.
The two runners cross the Point. They run into the village.
It's spring in Tikigaq. It's early summer.
The longspur, crane and phalarope are here.
The snow birds are warming their eggs already.
The longspurs are nesting on the tundra.
The young shaman disappears.
He'll dive headfirst through his grandmother's skylight.
She lives somewhere on the edge of Tikigaq.
That old aana's always lived there.
The young shaman has gone. He'll sleep all summer.
The men asked for their sleds.
The young shaman will send his aana's jaw-bones.
They'll use her jaw-bones to drag home their whale meat.

Nanmak heads for his umialiks' iglu.
He runs across the Point,
past qalgis and meat racks.
The dogs stand up.
They jump on their leashes,
All the dogs are barking.
The children have heard him.
They rush out barefoot.
He runs with his paddle.
They race behind him.
They are shouting and laughing.
'Qalualuraq! Qalualuraq!
The runner! The runner!'
The women come out.
They stand on their roofs,
they stand shading their eyes
on their iglu passages.
'It's Tikiq's messenger!

80

He's caught a whale!
  Tikiq's sent maktak from the flipper!'
Nanmak never stops.
  He reaches Tikiq's iglu.
The snow is thawing.
  He runs up the mound.
There is grass round the skylight.
  He circles the skylight.
Nanmak goes round once,
  in a sunwise direction.
Then he raises the membrane
  at its seaward corner,
and he calls into the iglu:
  'Here's fresh maktak!
Here's skin and blubber
  from the whale your husband's taken!'
The silence has ended.
  The hunt is over.
Tikigaq is noisy.
  The women climb out of their iglu passages.
They sing. They shout across the village.
  They pick up their knives,
they run to get their sleds and harness.

The women umialiks have been sitting in their iglus.
  While the men were on the ice, the women did nothing.
The umialiks come out.
  Their sisters and cousins, aunts and mothers,
girls and aanas all come out now.
  They've waited quietly in their iglus.
Now the women are laughing. They are ready.

A hand extends from its sleeve to the skylight. It grasps the paddle.
  'You have come! It is you!' The woman names Nanmak.
'From Tikiq, my husband! Our boat has been lucky!'
  The woman's voice is high and breathless.
The messenger picks off the long oval of maktak.
  'Aarigaa! Very good! Hand it down! We were hungry for whale meat!'
It is Tikiq's wife. Sigvana. Tikiq's hunting partner.
  'Now everyone can eat. We can all eat maktak!'
Nanmak passes down her wolftail mitten.
  He stands at the skylight. The children crowd him.

They swarm round the skylight.
　　They crane forward on their bellies.
'What kind? How big, Nanmak?' the children whisper.
　　The woman umialik calls up from the iglu.
'Children! Your *uncle* Tikiq has a whale.'
　　She calls Tikiq their uncle.
'He is with it on the ice. A big inutuq, or an usinuatchiaq.
　　He has sent me his paddle.
Now I'm going to cook this flipper.
　　When I come back from the ice, you will all eat maktak!'

Sigvana's voice retreats through the skylight.
　　It is time to get ready.
She dresses in her ceremonial parka.
　　She dangles the whaleskin over the lamp flame.
The black skin buckles; the fat turns yellow.
　　Oil drips in the lamp bowl.
She sharpens her knife and cuts the maktak into pieces.
　　The boys and young men start arriving.
Each boy has a rule his spirit guardian made him.
　　There are those who eat the first whale of the season.
Others eat the last whale to be landed.
　　Some boys eat seal meat in the morning.
They don't touch whale till the next sun has risen.
　　Some eat fresh whale.
Others eat it aged and frozen.
　　Some boys rub whale fat on their arms and bellies.
Others take it to their guardians.
　　They swallow the meat when their guardians have chewed it.
Some boys eat polar bear, seal and walrus.
　　Their guardians forbid whale in their first twenty winters.

The crewmen's women arrive at the iglu.
　　Sigvana gives them maktak and then kneels by a lamp bowl.
She holds her face above the lamp oil
　　and draws a soot line down her right cheek.
Then she draws soot across the left cheek.

Sigvana puts on her belt and her right-hand mitten.
　　She leaves her iglu with the qalgi women.
The women drag their sleds behind them.
　　Sigvana carries her qattaq of water.

She carries the paddle the messenger brought with him.
　　She has covered the blade-tip with raw caribou stomach.
She carries the last piece of maktak on the stomach.
　　They cross the Point. They walk down the beach.
They leave Tikigaq behind them.

The men stand and wait.
　　The whale floats at the ice-rim.
In turn each umialik
　　stands with Tikiq in his skinboat.
They talk and measure
　　with their feet and pole knives.

The old men advise them.
　　They cut lines along their portions.

Then the men take three paddles
　　and they make a tripod.
They lean three paddles,
　　blades up, on their handles.
Tikiq binds the paddles,
　　then fetches the whale's flukes
and lays them on the sea-ice
　　under the three paddles.

Then the women arrive.
　　Sigvana arrives with her qattaq and paddle.
She approaches the ice-rim.
　　She stands over the whale her husband has taken.
It's the same whale the Moon Spirit dropped in her qattaq,
　　last winter when she came out on her iglu passage.
Sigvana raised her qattaq, with the other women, through the sky-hole.
　　'Alinnaq!' she shouted. 'Drop a whale in my qattaq!'
She kept her qattaq in the iglu by the katak.
　　She kept the whale that the Moon Spirit gave her.
Then she sat in her iglu. She did nothing.
　　While the men were on the ice, she sat and did nothing.

That's how they caught it.
　　She sat at home and lured the whale to her.
She sat in her iglu, in the *animal,*
　　till her husband harpooned it.

She and her husband will send it to Tikigaq.
    They'll store its meat in the *animal's* body,
in the animal that Raven killed, whose body became Tikigaq.

Sigvana arrives with the qalgi women.
    She wears her ceremonial parka.
She hands back the maktak.
    She gives them the paddle.
The men slice up the maktak with the stomach.
    The crew eats maktak and caribou stomach.
Then the men cut holes in the ice near the water.
    They thread the holes with sealskin rope,
and raise the whale's head to the ice-edge.
    When the head is on the ice, Sigvana lifts her qattaq.
'Ii! Yes! *Quyanaq! Ii!* Yes! Thank you!'

            She cries 'Quyanaq! Thank you!
            You have come to my husband!
            You have come to our qalgi!
            You have come to join our people!
            You have come to Tikigaq!'

Sigvana lifts her qattaq.
    She pours water on the whale's head.
She gives the whale a drink of water.
    The water comes from a pond in Tikigaq.
The umialiks chopped ice there.
    Their wives kept it all winter.
A man made a whale there
    with a caribou-skin parka.
It was soaked in the blood
    of a woman who won't marry.
The men raped her in their qalgi.

She pours water in the whale's mouth.
    She pours water in the blowhole.
It is water from land.
    It is Tikigaq water.
She talks to the whale's soul.

'You died at sea!
Your soul must be thirsty!
Thank you for joining us!
Here is water!'

Sigvana has finished.
    She lays her qattaq on the whale flukes
under the three paddles.
    She takes off her parka and covers the paddles.

She walks to the skinboat
    and takes her husband's amulets.
She picks up the masks,
    the wolf-skulls and the effigies.
She lays the amulets over her parka.

The men turn to the whale.
    They sharpen their knives.
They get their meat hooks ready.
    They start butchering the whale.
The whale's body is dismembered.

Samaruna:
The whale hunt has finished.
The ice is floating north again.

Asatchaq:
'While the men cut the whale,
the boys and women drag meat to Tikigaq.

Samaruna:
They open their caches.
They line their old iglus.

Asatchaq:
The women start cooking.
They cook maktak for their qalgi.

Samaruna:
The children come first.
They run to their umialiks' iglus.

Asatchaq:
The children struggle at the skylight.
They throw soot at one another.

Samaruna:
The children drop spits
and pull maktak through the skylight.

Asatchaq:
Out on the ice the men finish cutting.
They haul the ribs and jaw-bones back to Tikigaq.

Samaruna:
The umialik cuts the whale's head.
He cuts it from the final vertebra.

Asatchaq:
The men cry out.

Satnaruna:
The skull meets the water.

Asatchaq:
The whale's soul escapes.
It returns to its country.

Samaruna:
They have finished.
They are happy.
It will find a new parka.

Asatchaq:
'Come again!' shouts the Raven.
The women repeat it.

Glossary

Spelling is in standard Inupiaq (north Alaskan Inuit) but with diacritical marks omitted. The pronunciation of most vowels and consonants is equivalent to the English. But:

Vowels
Short *a is* like u in 'cut'. Short i is like i in 'pin'. Short it is like oo in 'soot'. Short it before *q* or medial g is like o in 'hot'. Short i before *q* or medial g is like e in 'wet'. Long *a,* as in 'aana', is like short *a* but lengthened and stressed. Long i, as in 'ii', is like short i but lengthened and stressed. Long u, as in 'avataliguuvaq', is like short u but lengthened and stressed. All diphthongs receive stress, as in aana, inua, puiya, umialik.

Consonants q is a uvular stop, like a k pronounced at the back of the throat. The medial g, as in 'Tikigaq', is pronounced like a French *r.*

aana (ahnu)*	grandmother
agviq (urvek)	whale
anatkuq (ungutkok)	shaman
anaq (unuk)	excrement
avataliguuvaq (uvu-tuli-goovuk)	snow bunting
avataqpak (uvutukpuk)	float for whaling harpoon
iglu (igloo)	semi-subterranean winter house
igniruaqtuqtuq (er-ni-rawk-toktok)	amulet associated with birth-things
inua (in yoo u)	1) resident spirit; 2) 'human' component in animal soul structure
inugluk (inyorlook)	mask fitted to avataqpak
Inupiaq (Inyoopiuk)	north Alaskan Inuit, Eskimo
Ipiutak (Ipyutuk)	pre Inupiaq village on Tikigaq Point
Itivyaaq (Itivyaahk)	whaling spirit place and spirit person
katak (kutuk)	iglu entrance hole
maktak (muktuk)	whaleskin with blubber attached
nali (nulli)	Tikigaq's south shore
natchiq (nutchek)	hair seal
nigrun (nerroon)	animal; name for Tikigaq
nuna (noonu)	land
nuvuk (noovook)	point of land
puguq (poogok)	ceremonial carving made annually

* *Rough pronunciation is given in brackets.*

puiya (pooi yu)	lamp residue
qalgi (kul gi)	ceremonial house
qanitchaq (kunitchuk)	entrance passage
qattaq (kuttuk)	waterpot
qilya	shamanic power
qugvik (korvik)	wastepot
quluguluguq (kolorolorok)	old ceremonial carving
qunuqtuqtuq (kong ok toktok)	amulet associated with grave goods
taimmani (taym muni)	back then
taqsiun (tuk siyoon)	lure song for land animals
tatqiq inua (tutkek in yoo u)	moon spirit
tulugaq (tooloowak)	raven
tupitkaq (toopitkuk)	shaman's magical familiar
ugruk (oogrook)	bearded seal
uiluaqtaq (weel yawk tuk)	literally: 'woman who won't take a husband'
ulu (ooloo)	semi lunar woman's knife
umialik (oomaylik)	male or female skinboat owner
unipkaaq (oonipkahk)	old story
uqaluktuaq (okalooktawk)	ancestor history
usuk	penis
utchuk (ootchook)	vagina
yugaq (yooguk)	amulet dances

III Ancestors and Species

Note to the Reader

These passages are from a narrative poem written in 2000-01 about life and work in Tikigaq during the 1970s. I had been working for about seven years on a book about 19th century contact between Tikigaq and Euro-Americans, when Clio (muse of history) was kicked into the wings by one of her pushier young sisters and the non-historical pieces printed here forced their way out until I had to return the commissioned prose book (*Ultimate Americans*: 2007). I hope to complete the cycle with accounts of storytelling, local journeys, sea ice hunting and, in 1977, the arrival of TV.

While the past informs most of the loosely organised fragments published here, much of the experience recorded in these poems was comic. Over many months of visits, few days passed which did not burst, at some point, into hilarity, and I was lucky to find that I was a reasonable joker and could also supply involuntary exhibitions of ludicrous behaviour. The comedy sometimes burst in on the most solemn moments. The first experience of this happened on the morning of my arrival when I walked to a whalebone monument at one of Tikigaq's ceremonial sites and watched a flock of migrating whimbrels that had stopped to rest on some upright whalebones. This experience defined one point of entry: a silent, casual intersection of the past (the jaws of whales caught by long dead hunters) and what quietly passed through. In contrast to this moment, the trickster Uqpik, in whose house I had a few hours previously become a guest, had, while I was out, composed a greeting: his song about a gull which he imagined filling my upturned eye with its dropping (p.114). Uqpik's satire on a new white visitor travelled fast through the village, and by that evening the laughter it provoked had cut a second groove for me to settle into. It was helpful to learn this early in my work how casually the solemn and the comic co-exist with each other.

Asatchaq in Fairbanks

The events in the prose introduction take place in and around a nursing home in Fairbanks, Alaska, September 1975. Asatchaq, born 1891 in Tikigaq, is convalescing here after an attack of pneumonia. The writer has travelled to Fairbanks from Tikigaq and together they plan to move back to the village to record traditional stories. North Alaskan Inuit call themselves and their language 'Inupiaq'.

1.

Asatchaq's nursing home is at the edge of town off the highway to the airport, and sometimes on my way to visit, I stop at Macdonalds to fetch him a burger.

The old man's always hungry. Here in Fairbanks, 600 miles from his village on the northwest coast, he's starved of wild meat. *Niqipiaq* (real meat): caribou, whale, seal, polar bear.

'That's what I call it.' He thrusts out his jaw and grabs the Macdonalds with strong back teeth to trap it securely.

'These teeth,' he gestures one day to his canines, 'they're called *kiugitiik*. They're like a polar bear's. I always had these front teeth. Like a polar bear's. And when I was born, I never ate whale meat. Only *tuttu* (caribou) or seal meat. Until I was twenty.'

'Which *anatkuq* (shaman) put you in taboo?' I ask him. The old man cocks his head and squints. He drags the left side of his mouth down when he's thinking. It's as though, as he does this, broadening a screen within him, scenes and people enter. They've been sixty years gone. They enter fresh and lively. Then he projects them.

'It was Tiguatchialuk. He was the shaman. He showed my mother the three spirits at Itivyaaq. My father paid him. Gave him ivory and seal skins. He shamanized for us at whaling. When my father caught a whale in 1920 and they pulled it from the sea, they found the shaman's tooth marks on the flipper. He'd bitten that flipper when he visited the spirits. But when everyone ate whale meat, I ate polar bear . . .'

2.

It is mid-September and I've come down from the village. It's still hot in the interior. No one up there knew Asatchaq's whereabouts.

'He's having a rest,' was the neutral, sometimes guarded opinion. After all, he's 85, his breath comes short and his knees are crippled with arthritis.

Asatchaq is vague about the future. 'I'm going back. When you go back, we'll go back together. Then I'll tell stories.'

He's started already to prepare his recitations. Since our first meeting he appeared to have re-entered an otherwise abandoned history which reached back to the 19th century, then to myths and legends, which then with some difficulty curved round – as the myth world was packed off by contact with the white man – to meet the nineteenth century. Born at the end of his native tradition and the start of the first Christian dispensation, Asatchaq knew the values both embodied. And though feared and shunned by many in Tikigaq as the last of the pre-Christians, he was nonetheless respected as the village scholar.

In the meantime, this hygienic island, this pleasant, sunny, well-swept bungalow is his refuge. And to the white folks running the home, Asatchaq is just another pleasant-mannered ancient. Not that any resident's neglected. But their native past, in complex memories and opaque languages, is unreachable.

Inupiaq, Yup'ik, Gwitchin, Koyukuk, Tlingit, Ingalik, Aleutic. Most of Alaska's natives, Eskimo[1] and Indian, are represented here, living out their final days in virtual silence. Stranded in their rooms and in front of the TV, the old folk sit, in thrift-store shirts and trousers, like a patchwork map of tribes from a country the size of France and Scandinavia, and whose people, in their far-flung river and coastal villages, seldom meet each other except when they come to be cured of white men's diseases, or to die in comfort and isolation.

---

[1] The Eskimos of Alaska call themselves *Inupiaq* (singular: 'real person'), the equivalent of the Canadian Eskimo *Inuit*, but natives and non-natives still call Alaskan Inupiaqs *Eskimo*.

3.

As for me and this archaic stranger, I'm as innocent as the nursing aides and high-school kids who clean the room and change his linen.

I've spent six months in Asatchaq's village, and now it had taken me three more to find him. As I cycle from town in the late summer sun, it seems suddenly too easy.

'Jimmie? Oh sure! He's in Room 19. Turn straight down here and his room's ahead of you. He'll be real pleased to visit!'

I walk down the passage and stop briefly in the common room. *Charlie's Angels,* re-run for Alaska, is playing. A Yup'ik woman from St Lawrence Island, in a flowered calico parka-shift, sits curled in a wheel chair. Thick blueberry-coloured lines, tattooed on her cheeks before she ever saw a white man or an Indian, track through her wrinkles.

An old Athabascan from the Yukon River sits next to the woman. His eyes blaze with cataracts. He may never have seen a coastal Eskimo. His ancestors reached here eight thousand years ago; hers six thousand later. If they share any language and happen to talk, it must be in dialects of village English. She would be a Presbyterian, he an Episcopalian or Catholic.

4.

The door of room 19 is open. The old man's asleep. I stand at the threshold looking in on Asatchaq, or Jimmie Killigivuk. The name Asatchaq is from a shaman namesake who died the year before he was born in 1890. 'Jimmie' and the surname given by the missionary, comes from his father, Kiligvak, 'the mastodon'.

I hang there in the doorway. Bed, locker, armchair, Zimmer frame. Polished vinyl floor tiles. Behind the bed, a picture window. Birch, spruce, aspen, cottonwood and fire-weed crowd a rough lawn. Chickadees play in a dusty willow. Bees mumble rag-weed. A dragonfly shuttles through clumps of mosquitoes.

A generator thumps quietly in the background. The janitor in shirt-sleeves walks by with a metal tool-box. He's whistling a Dolly Parton number. A Monarch shimmers past him. Winter will freeze all this in a fortnight.

5.

Asatchaq is stocky, bow-legged, wears black trousers and white shirt. His short grey hair is neatly barbered. He sleeps curled with his right side to the doorway, shirt-sleeves rolled neatly. There's a walrus and anchor tattooed on the slack skin of his forearm and below the tattoo he wears a wrist watch. Black-rimmed glasses.

I call his name and Asatchaq half-rises, casts round for his slippers and adjusts his watch-strap. Then straight-backed and in quizzical anticipation, he recruits his awareness and extends a muscular right hand which grips mine softly. I think later of the work this hand has accomplished. The tons of meat, blood and fat it has harpooned, lifted, hauled, skinned and butchered. The nets and rifles, slings, snares, lashings, dogs and skin boats it has managed. The drummings, dances, rituals, sexual escapades it has engaged with. Now yielding and domesticated, this Inupiaq hand meets its would-be ethnographer.

'What's your name?' the old man asks me.

'Aniqsuayaaq,' I offer him in shorthand, hoping the name I've been given in the village will prompt his curiosity; and in this I'm lucky.

My good fortune lies in the power of the namesake. For the names of the dead, transferred to the living, revives and re-incarnates the ancestors' identities. To be given a kin name was thus to be in village history.

'Aniqsuayaaq!' growls the old man fondly. 'Who gave you that name? My father's harpooner was Aniqsuayaaq.'

I sit on his bed and we drift into silence. I give him village news and he digests it with indifference. Half an hour passes. I am doubtful of the future. Then the old man says suddenly: 'Sure. I'll tell stories. We'll go back together. We'll go home to Tikigaq.' When I rise to go home he scarcely seems to notice.

6.

White men are not new to Asatchaq. When he was born in 1891, there were whites already in the village. First, in 1887, came whaler-traders five miles down the beach at Jabbertown. Then Dr. Driggs, the missionary, arrived in 1890. Asatchaq's parents traded with the white men, but they didn't convert to Christianity.

When Asatchaq started school in 1900, Driggs gave Asatchaq a surname, after Kiligvak his father. Downriver, to distinguish him from other Kiligvaks, people called him *Kiligvauraq*: 'little mastodon'. Kiligvak died in 1925. Killed they said by a female shaman.

I close my eyes and think of the inlet north of the village, then paddling downstream in Niguvana's skin boat. From the high banks on the river, muddy *kiligvak* tusks dislodge and tumble. Months later, one sun-lit midnight on the north beach, I am pegging out a fish net and scoop out a fossilized *kiligvak* molar. It lies on the dark stones, golden and perfect, the surface sharply ridged for mashing and grinding Pleistocene grasses.

The first Americans followed mastodon, mammoth, woolly rhino, lion, elk and wild horse towards Alaska through Beringia.[2] When the glaciers melted about 15,000 years ago, the rising sea divided the new continents. The ancient beasts in both Eurasia and America fell victim to climatic change or over-hunting. *Kiligvak,* back then, was an animal both hunted and worshipped. Later, the Eskimos believed that they were giant, subterranean marmots. Nonetheless a powerful namesake.

7.

The road to the nursing home starts with a roar of traffic-dust, and peters out in scrub where the railway meets the river. This is the stretch I like walking or cycling. Town life dissolves. Willow, birch and meadowland with a scattering of little cabins take over.

It's quiet here and usually deserted. Who inhabits the small, tight houses in this dusty suburb? I wander round them. Spearmint, yarrow, willow bark, dried mushrooms stand in jars behind one window. A dog lies by the house-steps. A tiny, symmetrical spruce tree grows next to the kennel.

Besides herbal doctors there are also Buddhists down here. One cabin has green wax Bodhisattvas in the window, a wall hung with images of Tantric deities, and a neat row of incense burners in the form of laughing Chinese sages.

Then just across the meadow lives a family of pot-heads. In blue and white gingham, Darlene, on the front stoop sorts through berries, fixing up her winter pickles. Brad is home from a pipeline construction camp.

---

[2] The Bering land bridge and its surrounding territory.

He's made a miniature suit of medieval armour in the workshop. Halberd extended, the iron man guards an old whiskey crate from which grows a bush of marijuana fed by outhouse-oozings and mantric vibrations. A mandala proclaims *Om* in a lotus.

At the end of the road, the Department of Parks has converted some rough land to a baseball diamond, complete with link fence and a stand of benches.

Before cycling home, I watch women playing softball in the evening sunlight. Today is the final between Swann's Drilling Team and Friths Fossels. They are union workers from the pipeline companies: pipeyard women from the 'Over Thirty-five Geritol League'. Husbands, boy friends, children and colleagues lean on pickups shouting.

'O.K. girls! Let's play ball!
That's the way, Trudi!
Swing, Swing, Swing!
And Go! Go! Go!
Let's force the third! Swing, girls!
Stay ready out there, Trudi!'

Trudi, cropped and handsome, forearm bandaged, skies the ball into the wasteland. Two home runs, and the league's over for the season. The women crowd the trophies on the bonnet of a big Dodge pickup. A big man stands on the pickup bonnet and delivers a speech. Balls and fannies, cheers and whistles, punctuate his cheerful encomium. Trudi steps up to accept the first trophy.

8.

An ice-cream van painted with flaring utopian iconography stands in the car-port outside the nursing home. Planets, UFOs and Third Eyes float in a paradise of Himalayan temple-gardens. Wise men and female nature-spirits sprawl in the foliage round the driver's window where a bearded young man in army fatigues sits reading Zap Comix and smoking a Camel. Lured to the scene by Schumann's *Träumerei*, a girl limps through the swing doors, buys an ice, requests a cigarette, lights up and retreats. The ice-cream music switches to a lullaby by Brahms and the van drifts away towards the river.

9.

The track by the river twists through the scrub past some cabins where urban Inupiaqs have settled. They come here from the north to work as carpenters and electricians. Their families visit them; they move home to their villages; cousins and children travel down, and then others replace them.

This isn't a bad spot. They set snares for squirrels and rabbits in the brush near their cabins. Moose and red fox wander through. In the winter they fish through the ice on the river. I hope no-one bothers them.

Some afternoons I stroll round the lake in an old gravel pit. Owls take over from the loons and pintails in the early evening. I find pellets fretted with white scapulae and jaw-bones. Yesterday a rabbit skull. Caved-in but intact, it was stuffed with dried coyote excrement — its own digested, defecated self-meat, packed deep in its cranium.

10.

His English isn't good. My Inupiaq is rudimentary. The history is complex. I get tangled. It is late October. The window is dark and a folktale floats against it. I strain towards the old man, scrawling disconnected bits and pieces in my notebook.

Someone travels to the other side . . . East Cape, Siberia. There are fights, gestes, tricks and a shamanistic murder. Someone is flying. The traveller maintains a difficult posture. His amulet is a mythical creature involved in the killing. Retreats and counter-shaman visits. Tikigaq and East Cape swing unsteadily across the sea ice, requiting their losses and changing places.

All this is obscure and untidy. What Inupiaq I've learned comes quickly unravelled. Asatchaq's talk is involuted. I shift, sweat, stammer questions. Asatchaq is very disappointed. He knows how little I understand. He withdraws with a mean-looking sneer, returns half-heartedly, then drifts into silence. 'You should listen,' he growls, 'then you'll learn the story.'

If this was the moment he chose me to enter –
    the voices of forebears chiming through the mastodon's persistence–
the direction was obscure and the passage narrow.
    Had I trespassed already on some elder's arcanum?

The old man limped through Tikigaq nuna.[3]
    I followed dumbly. He tramped the north side through the beach stones,
stopping to name iglus [4] long since abandoned,
        their driftwood beams and whale-ribs jutting
through grass, saxifrage, anemones and poppies.
        In the mud-banks that had fallen we found stone points, fish-hooks,
bird skulls, relics of old ribs and vertebrae
        whose meat and oil had long been digested.

Asatchaq idled at graves marked by whale-jaws:
        Atanauraq's, Siuluk's, Talaaq's and Ayagiiyaq's.
These – beside his namesake – were village shamans.
        Wherever they'd gone, the trail their ghosts had carved was bony.
The track was contorted, spined with ivory and antler.
        Cold the access. Deep the strata.
'I'll give you their songs,' (his voice reluctant),
        stirring with his cane in the skeletal rubbish.
The ancestors' jaws lay in vaulted series,
        teeth cleaving to him and to me by proxy,
as the old man pointed down and inward.
                                    Such might be the journey.

Such, also, I feared was the old man's venture:
        the threat of some grimy, irresolute initiation.
For months I'd wandered the peninsula jaw-line.
        I knew its physiography, nomenclature and ritual places;
had mapped old iglus; plumbed a 19th century entrance passage.
        The thing was alive. The earth bristled with reminders.
The Point glowed with eroded whale-bone stubble:
        porous white and grey striated bowhead mandibles,
club-ended ribs and honeycombed and honey-coloured vertebrae.

Sealing the mouths of abandoned iglus on the bluff-edge
        where the whale boat owners cached their *maktak* [5],
lay walrus skulls, and fraying at their edges
        elegantly winged belukha [6] scapulae.
These were relics of the 19th century.
        Animals and humans mutually consorted.

---

[3] *nuna* = earth. Italicised passages, as here represent thought- or dream projections.
[4] traditional semi-subterranean house.   [5] whale skin and blubber
[6] white dolphin

At Uqpik's Cabin

Capping the ruins and scattered through the village stood the 19th century traders' cabins: tightly constructed clapboard houses with thick tar-paper insulation. Five of these houses, dragged back from Jabbertown[7] along the south beach in native skin boats, survived in the village.

Uqpik's[8] stood near the western end of the peninsula. It had been Max Lieb's cabin, bartered by his family when Lieb froze to death in 1902 on foot to the village from Cape Thompson[9] where he had been starving.

Lieb's house stood alone on flat ground near a grassy beach ridge, set round with iglu pits and their ruined whale bone tunnels. Still more remote, and infested with families of wild, nesting huskies, stood Asatchaq's cabin. Sixty years back, his father Kiligvak, 'the mastodon', had built it with lumber he bought from a Jabbertown trader — the first native frame-house in the village.

Perched near the south-west tip of the point, as though set to spring for the sea ice or the open water, the house, with its desolate window and broken chimney, was the furthest northwest building on the continent. Uqpik was its closest neighbour.

I'd stopped here, though the backpack nagged my shoulder,
    and watched a flight of longspurs feeding.
It was midday, and a hard wind rushed across the tundra.
    I was sweating and cold; my feet were swollen.
Still the outdoors held me.
    To enter this soon, was too soon, so it told me.
The south wind grew violent.
    It tore at the insulation on the corners which had broken
from their seams of deep, flat 19th century nail heads,
    buckling the east side where the dogs lay tethered.

I clambered up the northwest corner.
    Ox-eyed daisies, hinged to broken turfs around the house base,
rapped my ankles. Camomile tapped, as though knocking to enter,
    the edges of my boot soles.

---

[7] Late 19th century whaler-trader's settlement 5 miles from village
[8] 'Willow'.   [9] cliffs 35 miles south of village

Qanitchaq! Qanitchaq! [10]
As if no feet had ever broken through
the stepped frets of the labyrinth!

I glanced along the shed roof. There were caribou blankets
    pocked with thick eyes gnawed by warble-fly larvae;
some gulls, half rotted, plumage withered,
    beaks and claws in pieces, lay sprawled in a bundle.
Other remainders of game, traps, hunting tackle lodged here,
    anchored with long curving whale jaws,
and runners, like horns, of snow-mobiles, exanimate,
    stuck through some chassis that was rusting among discs and vertebrae.

A soul scuttled through the frieze of apparatus and detritus stored here.
    Torsos clamoured from the scaffold to retrace their bearings.
Midday winked. The fable mended. Red-fox-and-snowy-owl.
    They'd been just on the trail through their sublunary offices,
When the hunter – with an invitation for exchange and sociality – had
    detained them.

The fox squeezed out of his shriveled costume.
    He'd dressed in it only once too often.
Earth had grown skinny.
    No more fox tracks, no more ruckus.
Day ticked forward. Sun and wind rotation.
    The high disc shone through coat and muscle.

She'd been trapped in her nod, in her snow and soot plumage, [11]
    Eyes shrouded on his vertebrae,
His tooth on her shoulder, her beak on his sternum,
    Abrasively kissing, dialectically embracing,
Cross-hatched with each other,
    When death entertained and finally engaged them.

I tripped the latch, my thumb sliding on the runnels
    where eighty-five years of seal-oiled fingers
– hunters, Yankee-German traders, native wives and their 'half-breed'
    children –
had polished and unfixed the catchment.

---

[10] iglu entrance tunnel; frame house storm shed; traditionally locus of visionary events. [11] Evokes fable in which snowy owl and peregrine get speckled feathers when raven throws lamp soot at them.

It was twilight in the passage: the floor, defrosted tundra,
　　caving beneath plywood panels that squelched in the mash
and rocked from the centre as the inner door I sought emerged from the
　　dullness.

The horns of my backpack scraped a high shelf where I faltered,
　　wrenching the left shoulder, scapula extrapolated from its matrix
(on a photo-plate I felt it, geometrically projected) on the screen of entry
　　where I staggered to control the threshold.
　　　　　　　　　　　　　　　　　　　　　　Inside the room was black
as the tarp[12] I heard flopping and had seen it wagging from the east side
　　where the dogs slept flat-out in the grass, forget-me-nots and daisies.

The dazzle of that blazed outward to the window,
　　the scarred glaze of which gave back to the grass
and heaped lost rusting ironware: cans and barrels,
　　1950s pots and skillets, a discordant, dislocated aluminium kettle,
all the old American etceteras, accessories, disjected recent membra
　　scattered, half-sunk, stuck together –
itkaq was a verb I later gathered:
　　'to throw out, or abandon on the midden'.
Pah! I'm gonna itkaq this junk finally, I heard Suuyuk next year –

　　　　　　the dazzle of it rang, like brass splayed clean to brazen needles,
　　a clash, screwed-up, blazing musically
from the corners of the eyes which had dried in the wind-blast
　　and now tried adjusting to the darkness and its complex odour:
seal-oil, fuel, excrement and urine half-masked in a whiff of disinfectant.

There was a table where a pot of peanut butter
　　stood with a buck-knife handle sticking out of it:
twisted antler of the type you get from pawn shops
　　down in Sioux Falls, Laramie, Billings Montana, and on Fairbanks
　　　　2nd Avenue: masculine equipment.

Deep in the jar, the blade was set in folds of peanut butter,
　　the shrouds clotted with lumps of smashed peanuts and jelly:
while gazing from seal oil – golden, viscous,
　　in an emptied can of Skipjack tuna – I caught my reflection:

---

[12] Tar paper insulation

dust-fur on the tin's edge, spiked as the wolf-ruff
   of a parka hood, enveloping my hat and collar.

A sharp snore and the rattle of a sleeping-bag abraded my fixation.
   The thrash of nylon from a recess screened with plywood burst forth,
and a young man in an insulated boiler suit, grease-stained, ripped and puffy
   shambled from the bunk-space where he had been sleeping,
and with mouth half-open to receive his Winston,
   eyes doubly sunk in epicanthine ruins
– as though some clan-fate in a Kuniyoshi theatre vision[13] hatched his levee –
stood and watched me levering my pack down.

'You got everything?' the young man asked –
   as if, in courtesy, receding from a space once his,
in forethought he liked me without bothering to plot the detail,
   grasping that my presence, was some commerce of his seniors –
and went back to sleep behind his partition.
   'Okay,' I mumbled. I was irritated and embarrassed.
I wanted the whole cabin.

I settled my stuff and, disconcerted, primly looked round
   at the textures of the house interior.
There was gravel on the floor and table; the insulation on the walls and
               ceiling,
   webbed with soot from oil fumes, sagged dangerously inwards.
A near-century of grease from countless animals
   hauled up and butchered in the family circle gleamed
from every surface. Surrounding the peanut butter jar, on oilskin
   scarred by ice picks, knives and cigarette burns,
were sugar, sardines, tuna, jars of instant coffee,
   Pream[14], teabags and used teaspoons,
cogs, brackets, bolts and wrenches, screwdrivers and brake-wire:
   the truck of subsistence: abrupt indoor leavings
of out-of-doors business: meat, work and fuel of hunters and mechanics.
   A men's house. Uqpik's wife had died five years back,
and I missed her for them.

Next I was drawn to a length of gingham in the north-east corner:
   a rucked, shabbily suspended, hand stained curtain,

---

[13] 19th century woodcut artist of theatre prints.
[14] 'coffee-creamer'.

102

from which fumes of Lysol swayed through the twilight:
    the communal sump of several days' evacuations.

Converging here, as anthropologists had warned me they might,
    were all my prudery and learn'd aversions, masked previously
by bathroom culture, tiling, enamel and glazed sanitary polish.
    One glimpse of the crusted bucket-handle, and the clusterings, blurred,
of excrements half-melted at the loose brim of that dark infusion,
    and (impotent *in toto*, but to pitch in still quite anxious) I fled the
        house cringing.
Outside, the air was rough and simple.
    I walked to the beach and gratefully relieved my lower person,
though the wind shook my equipment, and a flurry of snow
    gusted down from the north which paralysed the sphincter.

*

A mist had come in and sunlight ran
in shafts and pieces through it.

Then rising on the Point ahead
was an arch of whale's jaw-bones,

two mandibles curving
against grey, half-hidden tundra.

The bones faced one another,
and their broad ellipse narrowed

at the high point without touching,
but stood open, enclosing in their tension

a long framed view,
through which, as I circled,

the village, sea and tundra,
were rotated: the tips of the uprights

vanishing in mist as though,
where it drifted in the sky between them,

the dead whale's vapour hung suspended:
breathed out to the faces of past hunters and women.

At the jaws' root in the long pale grasses
were three sets of tripods fixed waist-high:

whale ribs lashed in a ritual grouping,
where the skin-toss game

to celebrate successful whale hunts
was held in the spring time.

Then as I stood, I saw blow in
the flock of whimbrel.

There were eight, perhaps ten.
Streaked, mottled and lean-legged,

arched beaks drawing them
from somewhere they'd been feeding,

bills airily balanced
with the whale bone archways,

and cumbrously perched in calm
on their migration, they lifted and fell

slowly, in exchange of places
between jaws and tripods.

I counted again. There were eight birds –
nine, then twelve, now eleven –

enlarged and then shrouded
by fog in their plumage.

The wind dropped
and I heard them whistle,

gauntly piping, one to another,
a bleak call, but not scolding

as gulls and terns do, nor like
kittiwakes' incesssant weeping.

So they shuffled, fluttered,
appearing to flounder,

air to whale bone,
dropping

one, and then another,
shuttling their pattern,

and jumping across,
they wavered – idle slightly –

restless, in some exercise
of voyaging or ritual,

the purpose
of their long migration

and this point of repose here
                        inexplicit.

At Kunuyaq's

From Uqpik's I moved to another old black building. It was owned by some locals, but the school had been renting it, and since it was empty, Stubbs, the school principal, let me stay there.

Built by the trader John Backland in around 1920, the house had passed to Kunuyaq his local agent whose family maintained a store there till the 1960s. The house was on two floors – one of three in the village – which the school had converted to temporary classrooms, with big stoves up and down, and a picture window in the top room, below which was the flat roof of the storm shed with a ladder up to it.

On the day I arrived, Saul, Uqpik's cousin, was at work on the shed roof. It was March and he'd brought two bears in from the sea ice. Saul, like Uqpik, hunted almost daily, and both men spent the winter on the far ice, hunting polar bear. Even Asatchaq admitted they were knowledgeable hunters.

Saul was taller than his cousin, with a face battered by ice glare, wind and cigarette addiction. Unlike devotees of Marlboro or Winston, the Tikigaq preference, Saul's smoke was a Lucky, which lent to his slow, quiet, muscular manner, the aura of study and scholarly deliberation. It was as though the cork tip offered a mere amateur inhalation, whereas Lucky Strikes and Camels were the cigarette of ice technicians, polar bear masters.[15]

Saul was too busy to notice my arrival. But before going in, I stood with my pack and watched him nailing up the bear skins to dry above the storm shed. The skins were enormous. And seen from ground level, silhouetted in the twilight against the black tarp beside the upstairs window, they stood ghostly and colossal: guardians of some intermediate station which they occupied – Saul would clear two grand for them – between commerce and subsistence.

I settled in quickly, but logistics made me anxious. To fetch stove oil in drafts of fifty-five gallons involved hauling an empty barrel to the Co-op and then getting it home and installing it outside the building. Hauling

---

[15] Like scores of similar cigarette victims, Saul died of lung cancer.

water would be yet more laborious. Snow, polluted in its circulation round the village, was all right to wash in, but the only good drinking water came from pond-ice which lay five miles inland.

Toilet presented another problem but I stumbled on a pot half-buried in the snow wind-burned enough to be disinfected. The challenge was to get it down and outdoors ducking wind-sprayed urine.

The door to the storm shed was always tricky.
    The padlock jammed and the hinges were crooked.
Once I was inside, it took a minute
    coming from the snow-glare to adjust to the darkness.

Downstairs was a storage room that Kunuyaq and Backland had abandoned,
    unlit but for chinks of snow-light
through the clapboard of the north wall showing.
    So far as I knew there was nothing in the store room,
till one evening, with a flash light, I went in there,
    and saw hanging on the west wall, seal skin *maklaks*[16],
harpoon shafts from the 1950s, antiquated traps and fire-arms.

A rectanglar table, with heavily bulbed legs
    and inlaid with snow-drift filled the darkness.
I thought at first it was a grand piano.
    I flashed on Parkman's account of the mid-1840s,
of "shattered wrecks of ancient claw-footed tables,"
    and "cherished relics flung out to scorch and crack upon the . . . prairie."[17]
It was in fact a billiard table, hauled north, Suuyuk told me, in the 1940s.
    'All the men played then. Real good players.'

I'd watched young men at pool in Rock's Coffee Shop,
    self-confidently rolling with their sea ice cake-walk
round the table: denims and bandanas,
    outdoor-booted, quietly competitive,
but less to win than figure a trajectory,
    the likelihood of one uncertainty against another,
the slice, clack and negotiated tangent
    to the stream of movement,

---

[16] boots
[17] Francis Parkman, *The Oregon Trail*, 1849

a pure line tracked in spontaneity,
    shooting from the mind
across the intervention, space subverted,
    intersected by a maze of transitory angles.

They were casually so clever.
    As though to comprehend the longitude
of points at a distance were inherent
    in the eye-hand balance:
any swivel or contortion regulated
    by a small, quick adjustment,
so the bones were in alignment,
    ribs and pelvis sprung
in an elastic parallel,
    the body drawn like a compass needle
                      to its polar absolute.

In puffs of chalk dust, the clipped violence
    of breaks, shots, slams and ricochets,
glances off cue-ball streaking down into the pocket,
    was a hunt and dance-play,
dry, hygienic study,
    geometric diagram,
of relations they had known since childhood –
    along telescopic sights and rifle barrels –
with animals across snowy mountain-sides,
    wild fowl shearing down-wind in the twilight,
seals popping up in difficult currents,
    all things in the grain of habitat and movement,
and whose sudden appearances, so often awkward,
    demanded an instant counter intersection.

Most days I'd forage in the Co-op, fetch my mail, walk out
    to watch the sea ice, and pay visits to extended families.
For a time, till I quarreled with Stubbs and his second,
    I ate school lunch, and then told stories
that the elders had recorded for me to the elementary classes.

The children drew whales, bears, caribou
    and all the little animals that struggled through the ancient fables
for their space in the scheme of the early creation.
    How squirrels fought back against polar bears

that bullied them; how lemmings outwitted predatory owls and ravens;
     and the red fox was punished by the primal shamanness
for raiding her meat cache and not doing his own hunting.
     From deep in social memory and observation, the children drafted
lively, knowledgeable figures. They breathed quietly on their pages
     and out leaped back-lines of companion species,
bounding from the margins in spontaneous series: co-production,
     fabulous, *in nova . . . formas corpora*[18],
transformed to the present with their daddies in goggles
     on skidoos with sledges, and men in wool hats,
with cigarettes a-stream and shot-guns spurting.

Before nightfall I'd walk home, having multiply eaten,
     always famished by the time I'd crossed the village.
From the east as I approached the house,
     the blue forms, in the twilight, of the bear-skins
high above the storm shed greeted me austerely.
     Hair glowing darkly in the twilight
and packed loosely to the clapboard in a thick, sharp vanilla,
     it seemed they inclined stiffly to embrace me
(and my home inside which stood behind them), enjoining me
     to share, as I approached, their mute,
                              inconsequential crucifixion.

When I came home from the north side, they leaned,
     by contrast, in reverse direction, deep into the clapboard,
turning in their embrace, as though with their fur
     they cringed towards the insulation, ashamed to be seen –
by a white man even – empty, inside-out and internally naked.

As the wind beat onto and across their membrane,
     the flensed, red-flecked surface that the women had scraped
with their half-moon *ulu*-s[19], had dried crisp to a parchment,
     scoured down to the finest, inaccessible capillary:
as though Saul was preparing some manuscript vellum
     on which – where the scribble of veins
and a maze of intestines had recently figured –
     he might chart his own labyrinthine circuits.[20]

---

[18]Bodies into new forms: Ovid, *Metamorphoses* I.i: the theme of Ovid's 'unbroken song'.   [19] Semi-lunar women's knife.   [20]Alludes to the moon spirit, a hunter himself who controls hunting on earth, erratically wanders the sky, like human hunter.

Most nights I'd spend hours at an upstairs table,
    hemmed in by bear robes,
bracketed into that compound body,
    its twofold presence, open-chested,
thickening the north wall's insulation,
    hidden, except in occasional flurries,
when the wind came in a circle,
    and white-yellow bristles sprouted up and outwards,
horripilating grimly in the moon or the aurora.

Uqpik, whose house, due north, was visible,
    would sometimes emerge,
and walk quickly through the snow blur to the sea ice.
    Uqpik hunted alone, stayed out till nightfall and walked home in
            starlight.
When he sang they would come – or so,
    from his jokes and mutterings I would imagine –
and he'd talk to the bears, insult them, laugh, scold,
    light a Camel. Sometimes shoot one. Then leave them to it.

At Piquk's that winter, for the first time, I ate bear meat.
    Piquk cooked it at a fast boil in a great zinc basin.
Like boiled horse, it rolled in grey, heavy water,
    releasing brown suds and a granular bone-meal,
in miserable, humiliating scum which clung to the pieces.
    I liked seal, caribou and whale – meat, fat,
guts and stomachs, rutting, high, dried, raw, fermented, frozen –
    but I never could enjoy the long, tough fibres of a *nanuq*[21] filet,
the stink of its aborted energy spun-out through the whiff of propane,
    then defying the knife and rooting in the molars.

Still, to finish the evening we ate four of the bears' feet:
    delicate, translucent, shared out between eight of us,
separated with our knives and *ulu*-s,
    gristle trembling, gelatinous,
toes stripped to the yellow hour-glass of each metacarpal,
    the claws rattling on dinner plates, then swept into the garbage.

    That I sat here with their meat inside me
    And played jacks with their knuckles

---

[21]Polar bear

110

While they starved for self-life,
Struck me, as I studied
A dismembered lexicon
From a missionary's dictionary,
For the parts of the language
For parts of the body.

And thought from elsewhere
About karma[22] floated
Indecisively between Asia
And the present, in old remote
New World America, where all this
Reborn was unknowably translated.

'I've broken my tooth' said Uqpik near enough that day
  as we met in the morning at the Co-op checkout.
'Are you going outside to see a dentist?'
  'No, I mean the polar bear.'

'On frozen meat? I didn't know you ate it *quaq*[23].
  'The bear. She broke it. Maybe Asatchaq heard me.
He was sitting on a pressure ridge, and he listened to that *nanuq*.
  She was talking to herself because her tooth was busted.

Didn't you know I am a polar bear?'
  'I didn't. And you're not a woman are you?'
'No. But I had one last week. It was my birthday.
  Piece of ass from Silavik!'

The kinks snarled sharply and then came unknotted.
  He emerged from the story.
Asatchaq's tape, reeled smoothly in its cartridge,
  lapsed frozen and silent.
Where were the details? They lay on the carpet.
  Notes, tape, questions —
the haberdasher's box of field ethnography.

'That *uqaluktuaq*[24],' I started, 'of the hunter and the polar bear
  with tooth-ache . . . ' 'We don't listen much to those now,'

---

[22] Sanskrit: work; the consequence of action, leading to rebirth and the destiny of
species.   [23] raw frozen   [24] ancestor story

he reported, as if forwarding a message
    from his middle generation who had known them from their elders,
then disburdened themselves from the stress of too much ownership.
    'Let the old man tell you. I won't tell you.
By the way,' he continued, 'how many poems have you written?'
    And then: 'Here's one of mine. It's for you and about you.'

        Tom Lowenstein came to Point Hope.
        He went down to the beach.
        And he looked up at the sky.
        Sea gull shit in his eye.

Can I borrow your cheeks?' he went off. 'Mine are frozen.'
    By now when I'd cleared the figured shit from my eye,
I'd totted up the poems I'd written.
        There were forty-six, not counting a prose sequence.
I'd been just about to tell him.

'Those polar bears know me,' Uqpik went on, later.
    And I'm not afraid of them. But they all know me.
Once I went out with Agniin, my sister.
    We were on the sea ice — straight out there,'
pointing to the north side, towards Cape Lisburne.
    'Where's your rifle?' asked my sister.
'I don't need a rifle. Those polar bears know me.'
    So we went out further. Came to an *ivuniq*.[25]
'There's a polar bear behind that ice,' I told her.
    She believed me. She knew hunting.
Then I shouted to it. Called out loudly.
    Polar bear was sleeping maybe.
Then we heard its feet on the snow. And grunting, breathing.'
    'Come on,' said my sister. She wanted to go home now.
'It won't eat you. I'll tell it not to eat you.'
    Then that *nanuq* came round. It was quite a big one.
Mean and skinny. Sick, I guess. Hungry.
    It'd been in a fight. Got hurt by a walrus,
maybe in its belly. That's when I started.
    'Don't eat her!' I shouted.
'Come and eat me!' '*Arii!*' said my sister. She was scared by this time.

---

[25] sea ice pressure ridge; a raised spine of ice.

'When it's eaten me, it'll have you for its supper.'
She turned her back and started to walk home.
　'All right,' I told the *nanuq*. It could understand my language.
'That's my sister. I will *malik*.[26]
　She doesn't like you. But I'll come back later.'
Damn' if that *nanuq* didn't walk back behind me.
　I stopped a while and tried to help it.
'Go and get yourself some seal meat.
　Then I'll come and find you.'

***

The Children Call Across

My first name in those early weeks at Kunuyaq's
　　was redefined, too, in the form of a shock
as issued to me back from children
　　I had come to know in school hours
when they started, in a gleeful trace, to hunt my day-pack,
　　as I walked to the south side, home to spend time
with books, tapes, letters, language exercises,
　　and not least the viola – Bruno Barbieri's from Cremona –
which I'd brought north, absurdly, to practice Bach's 3rd cello suite,
　　and, in preparation for the Brahms sonatas[27], 4th position studies.

I walked home anxious for a quiet I'd imagined
　　on my trip through America:
London growing paler as I'd travelled from New York, Chicago,
　　West, and then here to the Arctic,
the kernel of one in the husk of another,
　　and dimming as the moon wears down –
till gibbous, smeared bone – gives out finally
　　in twilight too thin for the emptiness even.

I'd imagined a solitude and quiet people:
　　a reduction beyond needs I'd been shouting to feed
as recently as Friday evening:
　　　　　　　a bone of non-ego, I'd thought, glowing
　　at some antithetic parallel,

---

[26] Follow her.　　[27] The Clarinet and Piano Sonatas, op. 120 arranged by Brahms for viola.

purified by elementals and Arcturus' vigil,
    clean of self-meat, bare with an existence present,
and that roar of the human from the marrow outwards,
    with its pleasures-schedule,
the subconscious newsreel dark with past non-fictional eventualities.

And thus I'd visualised my Arctic *kuti*[28]
    defined by the tranquil walls of a cabin,
a few serious books, my paraffin lamp,
    with now and then some ethnographic *conversazione*,
in deep alliance with respectful others
    as we listened to the wind
and conjured the forebears,
    musing on change, the temper of duality,
and what, as I made tea,
    with vain servility, were self and essence,
and how live without women.

'Now here's a fine text', I could hear myself in further sub-plot
    rapping off some embers from my meerschaum,
as I worked up dottle before tamping in
    with masterful but kindly thumb-print
cured discs (specialities imported), and lounging back then
    in a twilight which the blue smoke hallowed,
and thus offering my weight to silence as the syntax
    concertinaed from the left side to its colon: —

'Our Asatchaq's tale – homologised with variants
    from southern forest people as published by Strauss
in his first great volume – conveys a tone
    all tribal memories, I think, imprint on mythic narrative.

I mean, for example, that your wandering trickster,
    whether among sea ice or the great plains hunters, the carnivorous,
nocturnal skunk of central Amazonia their shamans transform to,
    or a monkey Buddha, even, with detachable phallus
tall, dense and hard and useful as the product of the ironwood forest:

    such figures, I hazard, tell us something
of those universal energies we all seek, don't we,

---

[28] Pali: hut for Buddhist contemplatives

114

to appease, cultivate, transfigure
in our psycho-spiritual development?

It's there, too, isn't it, in stride piano —
    think of James P. Johnson's tramping
left hand octaves, Teddy Wilson and Earl Hines's riffs,
    the older Count Basie: trickster-shamans, every man of them:
cantering, meandering their muskat ratty ramble:
    Coyote, Old Man, Hare and Raven – they wuz **going** *–*
the lolloping onward of Brer Fox and Rabbit[29],

    or that formless pre-human **lolajatika**, *non-embodied* **atta** *(being),*
who rolled, lolled, schlepped and trucked and shambled,
    on fresh, warm milk-crust of its latest cosmic evolution,
scooping **bhumi rasika**[30], *with not-hands*
    of first being to become becoming,

and grabbed up sweet quintessence, whence –
    the wet delectability of earth crumb mouthing –
all our woes *come,*
    and this infantile taboo transgression horror!'

Tangled (in pursuit of is-ness)
    with the furor of becoming,
there was truth perhaps in more than one condition.
    But that I was myself still,
more or less as previously conditioned,
    I knew — as those children found and nailed me
to a long entrenchment in my own strait corner,
    and *they* knew, perhaps, the comedy was deeper
than I might imagine. We were playing all over. I hated to guess this.

From school, its blue wall at our back, the way was beaten,
    the snow ridged as they toppled me over,
shouting my first name spelled out tri-syllabically,

---

[29] All these figures are versions of the Native American trickster-shaman who roamed the early world, transforming, through greed, transgression, creative will, the phenomenal world to its evolved form. From *Uncle Remus* stories, Brer Fox and Rabbit derive from south-east native American tales which converged with African traditions introduced by American slave populations.   [30] *lolajataka* is a trickster of Pali literature who, after tasting the milk-rice crust of 'edible earth' (*bhumi rasika*), set in motion the materialization of previously joyful 'mind-fed' fellow beings.

115

so I came, in dismay, to be their monster and their curiosity,
fugitive and mascot, gadget, rugby lozenge,
    as they fell on my legs and floored me in the sharp dry snow-crust
till it rasped on the throat in our multiple skirmish:
    which was reasonable fun and pleasantly good humoured,
whilst intermittently abrasive, as if shaving
    long raw patterns with a cold blade as the scrum pushed forward.

All they wanted was to visit my apartment
    – 'Can we visit?' sweetly, pipingly entreated, lame albeit sadly
in translation of a noble verb-stem[31] binding host and visitor
    to a mutual courtesy of meat and quietness,
with the confidence, too, of future reciprocity –
    and now that I was winded,
I had scarce a civil or coherent paragraph
    to forestall their entrance, nor any good reason.
So they rumbled up the staircase,
    ready and ordered on the landing in a horseshoe,
where my things neatly waited,
    and I tramped in after,
a bit snow-burned, with my goggles dragging.

The children's visits went on through the six weeks before whaling.
    They came most days, and when I was out,
or I wouldn't answer, they threw gravel in snowballs
    at the downstairs window and then one day broke it.
There were about ten, and sometimes
    a girl would *amaaq*[32] a baby niece or sister in her parka,
and we'd have nappy crises.

The visit their first evening had gone smoothly
    to start with. They tried out my camera and cassette recorder,
vaguely handled Bruno Barbieri, attended politely
    when I sawed them a bourree, and got going with *Booster*,
a dice game from Chicago's western suburbs in the post-prohibition 1930s,
    converted for an English fairground to take old pennies.
I had some coppers – worn George Vs and Queen Victorias:
    dark and glossy: thin they'd ripened –
and they rang, when you spent them through a tongue into the workings,

---

[31] *isiqattaaq* — 'pay a social visit'.   [32] Carried babies on their backs inside their parkas.

116

bright from down the cavern of the oak box,
as the fruit dice flew on a spinning green baize table,
    and their edges flicked and gibbered on the glass plate
and then settled, although loaded by hoodlums into losing combinations,
    in juicily clashing, or the sweet virtual harmony, of bells, oranges
                and cherries.
Nothing was stolen or defaced or broken,
    and I started to like these children as they kept themselves in order,
as though here was a clubroom with a stalwart leader to look up to,
    who had new things for them to extend their skills experience,
so 'Don't touch that, Arnie,' came from their seniors,
    whose task adopted was to legalise the boundaries and interpret.
Not that our lingos differed beyond latitudes of dialect,
    though their pride when they showed that they could
count to ten in Eskimo made me wretched and embarrassed,
    and to hide my chagrin I spun them a tape I'd recorded last autumn
in the stockroom cupboard of S. Hackney where I'd covered for remedial
                reading:
    it was Mavis and Donna in Well Street market **tirra-lirra**,
singing *Inky-pinky-ponky*, *Colonel Bogey*, *Maresy-Dotes* and *Dozey-Dotes*
    bowing out thro' lorry traffic roaring east with *My Old Man's a Dustman*,
and it wasn't too long, though I never tried to teach them,
    before the Kunuyaq kids
could *parlay-voo* with the Bisto children, confidently chirping:

        'e wears a dustman's 'at
        'e wears gor-blimey trousers
        and vat's the end of vat.[33]

I quite enjoyed my station as their wizard,
    dozing serenely in an acquiesence mesmerised
with the collective blank we shared together.
    At first everyone whispered; moved round with discretion,
guessed with each other where, like them, I was a native.
    They quizzed me of trees. If Eskimos could live in London.
Whether we had *taaqsipak-s*[34]. Which animals 'my people' hunted.
    If you got *qaaq*[35], and how much was it.

---

[33] 'Not *that*, kids. *Vat*. *Vat!*' I confess directing them, reversing elocution lessons cockney mothers wanted me to help with in the 1960s. [34] black people; lit. 'those who have become dark'. [35] marijuana; literally: the verb 'explode'.

They wanted to know about my mother: name and function.
    If I had a girl friend. And what kind, then?
'Do you always *kuyak?*' was another question,
    meaning, I learned – when they glossed the query with their palms
and fingers, hinged from wrists which they joined at the pulses
    and with gaping palpitations – was 'to have sex with'.

The word 'always' in their conversation puzzled and annoyed me.
    We ate crackers, Salteeners and peanut butter.
'Do you always,' pronounced *allus,* 'eat this kind?' they asked me.
    'Not *always,*' casually at first I answered,
and then with rude, sarcastic stress which was callously offensive,
    I waved my arms and shouted, 'Of course I *always kukak,*'
(still couldn't say it), '*always* eat peanut butter, *always* do everything . . .[36]'

They laughed my outburst
    but I didn't get why.
So I strained myself to joke them
    and tried extending the entertainment
to compensate for my impatience.
    Their visits grew longer,
more hostile and imperative.
    They wanted to have things,
ran round the room
    with my goggles or the camera:
'If you want it,' swinging it,
    'you catch me',

then started to curse my habits and my person,
    that I *couldn't share food* and would *steal their language,*
which had happened, I agreed, already,
    and like them, I knew for the shame they endured
from their scolding elders, that I wanted to learn it.

To this the riposte: 'How come you write poems?'
    For my labours grew visibly in solipsistic self-importance,
with piles of carbons, apothegms and footnotes for the Booster system,
    e-s and o-s I'd punched through the middle on my Olivetti,
they'd pick gingerly clean, then:

---

[36] I understood later that 'always' is a good translation of the infix *-suu,* meaning 'habitually to' + verb.

'Try see!' came a shuffle, the bunch craning inward,
and tracing the braille their grooming had perfected,
    they'd read through my latest, and I must digest
their too-justified satire or weary them
    with paraphrases of the nonsense I was writing.

Anonymous at first in all but Biblical or English *atiq*[37],
    I soon learned their parents, whaling clans and houses,
and while anxious to say nothing,
    when once in a moment fraught with dread and terror,
I whispered something to an old pal I was out with:
    We're freaked out, lots of us, he muttered, *by these children.*
'What should I do? I squeezed up from my muddle,
    aware of Bunyan vaguely,
but without the moral interest which might justify a helpful answer.
    Narrowing his lids, my guide blinked lightly.
We were on the sea-ice and these seals to drag home was all his business.
    If we hurried he could get the sled back without having to jump water.

While I sat at a *desk*, could I name the things *work* there?
    First-light fell from the north side in metal,
tingeing my verb-lists with a grisly winter aluminium. Then, p.m-s,
    when the children stood here, an intensifying charcoal swept through,
blue dust filling ineluctably with dregs the twilight filtered
    till it sank us in that overwhelming particle,
and their cheeks and foreheads glowed, strung nebulous in moons,
    with hood-ruffs floated copper on warm hairy circles.

A moment came when my things went haywire,
    as though tension inherent in irritable feelings,
given the thin texture of my patience and their desire for the privilege
    I represented and provisionally implanted here, exploded.
All my systems – camera, SONY, goggles, little Olivetti, notes, cassettes,
                and Booster pennies – were in action,
    and the whole room spun, the hurl syncopated and the muddle circular,
the stuff I'd come with and relied on all went sickeningly whizzing
    in directions that I couldn't follow, though my cries and stamping
tried to fix down artefacts as they whirred into view, then off again
    beyond the eye-tail and amalgamated one into the other,

---

[37] *atiq* = name. Everyone has a Euro-American or Biblical name as well as an Eskimo name. I couldn't say these yet.

119

straps and packing, leather cases tangled,
    shuttling like coleoptera, black shards flapping on their hinges,
not humming as on drowsy nights in nether latitudes
    but thwacking, rebarbative, refracted –
while through the confusion and singing unheard to the spirits of the
            weather,
    came Geza Anda, directing with great spirit, the 'Elvira Madigan
            concerto'.[38]

'We'll come back,' someone shouted when they'd filtered off by sunset,
    'because we always visit,' and their promise of *always*
rang across the packed snow, as if they'd announced a recurring series:
    I would *always* live here, they would *always* be ten,
and more and more, as the months crept along, would qualify to be my
            visitors,
    returning with new cohorts,
selected by rota, and in alternating *qalgi*-s, from each coming generation.
    So that night when they'd gone, I improvised a lock:
a clumsy devise of some binding I'd found and a nail on the door-jamb,
    and dozed queasily to *Panama Red* by Peter Rowan.[39]

They returned around midnight,
    as though on some long, animated leather apparatus,
like the stones of a bolas, flung out from their scattered houses
    and boomeranged in phalanx through the village,
came springing to the house front,
    wrapping, as they might some big, dark, stranded creature,
the downstairs of the house, its storm-shed, walls and windows.

The outer door, unhinged at the top, hung gaping half open,
    but my inner defensive catch-contraption held,
and they didn't dare batter a passage through it.
    So they hammered instead on the inside entrance,
and two boys swarmed the storm-shed ladder
    and capered satirically at my window.
'Let us in,' I heard from downstairs, hoarsely.
    'No you can't. Go away. It's late. I'm working.'
'You're crazy,' someone shouted. 'He hates Eskimos,'
    I heard another. 'Let's bust in the *qanitchaq*.[40]

---

[38] Mozart piano concerto K.467.   [39] From the album *Old and in the Way*, with David Grisman and Diego Garcia.   [40] *qanitchaq:* storm shed

The two on the roof glued their eyes to the window,
    lips turned out in crustaceous suckers,
sideways crawling, and masks smeared flatly,
    goggling my books and papers.

'Fuck off,' rose feebly, and it balanced on the larynx,
    half-up, like a vomit which had tentatively risen,
but which fell without disgorge,
    leaving the throat burnt with systemic acid,
while chemicals of terror raked through the tissue,
    as though waves flushed, climbed and then receded,
to leave alkaline deposits on the cerebellum lining,
    and crusted the primary nervous functions.

The children had arrived as I was juggling two pots of urine.
    My chamber pot was brim-full and I'd taken it downstairs,
with a view to discharging the contents in my barrel next morning,[41]
    and make do with a fruit-can I had finished.

I crawled back up crab-wise and turned the light off.
    Outside, there was running.
The *qanitchaq* rumbled –
    then their feet like mosquitoes,
hsk-hsk on the standing crystals –

Downstairs next morning.
    stooped gingerly across the freezing *qanitchaq*,
and opened the front door to let in daylight.

There were the billiard-table, traps and harpoons,
    the worm-eaten pairs of *maklaks* [42] shrivelled —
Aber: wo ist meine nette qugvik? [43]
    I smiled at the mystery. Had the children, I considered,
done service beyond duty, and taken out my *qugvik* –
    'He's given us so much. Let's *itkaq* [44] for him, this once, maybe!'–

Aber nein: there it lay on the floor-boards, tipsily angled –
    initially a frisbee? Then I flashed on a bowler –

---

[41] Empty 55-gallon oil drums for domestic waste stood outside most houses. These were rolled to the sea ice after whaling, where they sank during the thaw. [42] *maklaks*: boots. [43] *qugvik*: urine pot, to which I have attributed the feminine. [44] *itkaq*: throw out

a toy from *City Lights* – some circus outfit – until gouts of the slush
    that drooled from the cusped lip
sprang into focus — the folded, warm 'last oozings',
    fringed in citrine: crystalline, translucent, shaggy.

I glanced up then. Shafted by the doorframe's *camera obscura*
    (the splash intensified by vitamin supplements my mother'd
        recommended)
congealed on the uprights, the inner door had been translated.

It was no dream. I stood broad waking. There shone the star,
    As conceived in the ghetto, points radiant on the door posts,
a corrupted *mezzuza*:[45] hypertrophied, the Magen David –
    Saul's bears wincing, *traef* [46] pinned up here –
And could eavesdrop no harp songs even if I could remember.

★★★

---

[45] The Hebrew verse dictates that 'thou shalt bind [a sacred injunction] for a sign upon thy hand, doorposts, and upon thy gates . . .' A *mezzuza*, a small containerised scroll fixed to the door-frame of a pious household, is a materialization of this command.
[46] Traef: non-kosher food.

122

At Jabbertown — 1890
for John R. Bockstoce

In reaction to my negativity towards the children, I sought the roots of
their behaviour in a period of traumatic dislocation as a result of contact
with white men during the 19th century. The focus shifts to 1890 when
commercial whalers created a cosmopolitan community known as
Jabbertown five miles south of the village. Jabbertown lasted from 1887
to about 1914 when the bowhead whale had been almost hunted out and
spring steel replaced baleen (whalebone) for corset construction.

Besides the Yankees, there were Germans,
    Irish, black men, a few Kanakas[47]: the frontier rabble,
'lowest sweepings' out of San Francisco's water-front saloons –
    feared and detested by the Protestant domestic missions –
unchurched 'squaw men' who sowed mayhem
    in the mining camps and hunter/trapper stations,
doubly corrupting Eskimos and Indians
    whose *savage natural innocence*
was thus more deeply *paganised* by frontier manners.

Still the Eskimos quite liked white men, found them useful
    and amusing. They pragmatically grabbed
each opportune convenience and expedient for subsistence
    brought them to replace resources that the white man
destroyed with explosive harpoons and repeating firearms.

They stayed ethnically self-centred. The moon,
    whose spirit lifted off one winter,
taimmani[48], from Tikigaq, the criminal moon who'd raped his sister
    and who hunted in the lunar ice fields,
giving sublunary hunters all the game they needed
    or deserved by paradoxical propitiation,
the contradictory *tatqiq*[49]
    was still focused on the sharp tip of the village —

its light poured in a line directly to the whale-blood of the 'animal'[50]:
the harpooned beast whose wound-scar from the Raven harpooner

---

[47] Hawaians. Hawaii was a supply centre for New England whalers en route for the
Japan grounds.   [48] 'back then' in myth time.   [49] moon   [50] *'the animal'*, alluding
to the mythological transformation of the land from a sea-beast, was one of the
Tikigaq people's names for the peninsula point.

still lay here on the grassed turf of a beach-ridge,
     reiterating and proclaiming the archaic shaman's strike,
and refracted by association with the counter-trickster,
     in its sacrilegious lunar separation,
deriving its rough order from taboo infraction,
     and which rendered land and people
(victimised and perfect) dangerously sacred — [51]

thus identifying, in the shade of the archaic layers,
     through which mind conflated dream with day-thought,
the Inupiat as *real* because they'd always lived
     within this semi-self-created system:
and others from elsewhere lay beyond
     the consecrated centre, and were not quite *people.*

If myth was the substrate, recent history was co-present:
     the who and when of several generations fixed
the current of each momentary and successive context,
     quick lives fleshed in lamp and kayak dialects,
and with a quick laugh summarized as landscape,
     theirs in the maps the elders had adjusted
to their own long, now abbreviated storm days.

In the middle distance, then, the last routines of purely local
               reminiscence
     with horizons uncorrupted and uncluttered:
                              but now on the skyline
there came cross-hatched structures, masted and then also funneled,
     the scaffolding a-bristle, sketched in complicated silhouette
as though each rig were bird bone and sinew dried and lifted,
     or disjointed from the meat part
in some planally disorganised arrangement,
     a great wing flexing erect its exo-skeleton,
and then as the ships closed, they saw marvelous
     hypertrophies of skinboat and fantastication,
alive, alone, aloof and curiously peopled,
     heavy with stuff indefinably desirable,
 but then abruptly gone in atmospheric summer shimmer.

Children stood on the shore,
     their boots rattling the beach stones

---

[51] References are to the creative/destructive trickster shamans of myth whose taboo infractions haunt Tikigaq's origin stories.

that were mixed with spindrift fragments
      and spots of Silurian fossil flora
in washed blue granite:
      they watched the big ships in the mist consolidate:
their lines solidifying gradually more brittle,
      like dust in cloud light,
something complex at their centre coming
      for them: as though iron and carbohydrate,
with their outriders of nicotine and liquor
      were some hazy *tupitkaq*[52]
constructed from detritus of the white man's tackle,
      with a bio-spirit likewise mingling
in arbitrary bric-a-brac, the epidemic viruses
      which spun from the hale breath
of San Francisco and New Bedford whalers:
      the spirits of measles, flu and whooping cough
in synchrony with scarlet fever, syphilis,
      diphtheria and meningitis, microbally alive,
invisible, incurable, incomprehensible:
      it was coming for them with the men
who would smile and maybe kiss them,
      and whose breath leaped out,
with sometimes *membra virilorum,*
      to cut down every generation in the village.

They were phantoms with eye-brows,
      not *genuine people,*
with beards, hats, buttons, red ears (big ones)
      high boots and waistcoats,
grey complexions, veined and whiskered,
      noses variously sharp and stubby,
which like knives and their chins
      ambitiously cut forward,
brains working through their blue hats,
      single-minded on some project
which forged straight lines
      into trade and commerce,
not circular, colluding
      with the game migrations

---

[52] a shamanistic figurine of bones, skin and sinew made for the purpose of supernatural assault.

or translating the contour
    of an obligation to the animals,
but killing for those parts
    they could exchange for money.

On the south beach where the shore-based whalers settled, I'd walked out
to inspect some graves set back on high ground they called Beacon Hill
between the beach, lagoons and tundra, above Jabbertown where Koenig,
Hachmann, Max Lieb, Bayne, Tom George – a black man – and the courtly
Jim Allen wintered, pushing their skiffs through the spring ice to hunt
bowhead, polar bear and walrus. Crushed to starvation, the Tikigaq men
still disdained to work the *naluagmiu*'s[53] whale boats, so the whites fetched
people from the river villages who settled here, competed with the locals
and inter-married.

The grass on these graves was exhausted from their eighty winters
    and snow capped in lumps its arched extremities,
but the grass supported two small picket fences,
    each lath-head angled poignantly,
enclosing the ecclesiastic plots where Lieb and his partner
    lay embalmed in permafrost, their ornamental crosses darkly rusted,
while the shaman Talaaq – who'd come from the Kobuk
to work at Beacon Hill in 1900, and who died next spring
    as he paddled his kayak, floating peacefully all day,
a pipe of baccy frozen in his *rigor mortis* – lay off centre.

        You only had to cut the turf
    on Talaaq's grave and turn it,
        to reverse the wind's direction.

        I'd tramped round Jabbertown,
            put a tent up in the grass
        above the fringe of driftwood
            separating beach and tundra,
        sat nights with *ugruk* hunters
            with a blaze of birch, spruce, cottonwood
        swept upcoast from the southern rivers,
            sun low at midnight,
        and a south wind beating —

---

[53] White men

We chewed fresh *paniqtaq*[54],
    which sprang twisted and elastic
off the knife-blade
    to the jaws that worked them,
and which painfully split
    between the canines and incisors,
and then loosened the throat with *ugruk* blubber,
    drank hot black tea,
staggered off to *anaq*[55] —

    the face bathed sometimes
    as you squatted
    suddenly in honey
    on the wind from
    campion or saxifrage,

burying the faeces,
    dry, forced and black
as dried out twisted seal meat,
    in stones, sand, mica-grit and beach grass —

It reminded you of many stories:
    Utuagaaluk, for example,
who couldn't reach
    the long grass that he needed
as he cast around to wipe his *itiq*[56],
    to find as he shuffled, the toes
of his dead cousin that his
    sakigaq had murdered,

or Ukunniq, on this same beach
    dipping supernatural whale-bone wedges
in his *anaq*[57] so the wedges wouldn't
    knock his head off when he used them
to split logs with . . .

So these stories bound the small hours
    as we watched the floe-ice,
bruise-purple-cloud-in-yellow-sunset,

---

[54] wind-dried meat   [55] defecate   [56] anus   [57] faeces

crowbills[58] low across the open water
in long urgent lines of feeding adults,
        eider duck and old squaw roaring
to their nests behind us on the marshes,
        knots, snipe, small owls,
phalarope and plover,
        sandhill cranes in thoughtful
couples from Chukotka,

Or we filched the children's comics,
        read 'Richy Rich'
and his shaman butler
        plagiarised from P.G. Wodehouse,
then slept in the morning
        when the sun grew warmer,
till the men strolled out
        and hunted on the rotting floes
for *ugruk* and walrus.

I combed the beach and headland
        for some residue of Jabbertown,
some clue, inscription,
        hardware, trace of a foundation,

but the white man had gone: his place was flush
        with the contour of the bluff,
which was scoured by south wind,
        rhythmically levelled since 1914

by the tide and current:
        there was nothing of Jabbertown
just the bones
        of animals hauled up
on the beach-head,
        eroded with each pass of weather:

some hollowed
        soft white morphs
whose cusps and whorls
        and broken edges

---

[58] guillemots

were sanded by the wind
        or water-eaten,
a joint and its socket
        empty at the centre
of the vortex where the air
        stopped at the apex
of the wind's attenuation
        and came finally to nothing.

Here and there
        was something larger and more heavy:
the bones of a walrus or an *ugruk*[59],
        ribs sprung in the grasses
and with saxifrage or beach pea
        sprouting through
the interstices of a clavicle
        or vertebra –,

the whiteness flaking in short
granular splinters, or a whale's disc
filled with crumbs of tundra mosses –

as if beasts
        had hauled
up-beach here
        to evolve near Tikigaq:
but dragged
        themselves no further
than the early century.

Then I found what I'd been hunting:
        it lay in the stones,
the bracket thinned from a crust of its blisters
        which the salt had opened:
                        a vast hinge
from some 19th century foundry
        between Pittsburgh and Lake Erie, maybe,
rollers seized-up, but the screw holes
        clear and still visibly bevelled.

---

[59] bearded seal

So I lugged the thing back and put it on my table
　　where it sat among paperbacks, tapes and carbons, shedding slowly,
dislocated twice now from the rising body of America industrialising:
　　Pennsylvanian iron-works forging Jabbertown's
then Tikigaq's harpoon irons:
　　the ice hunt protracted from that workshop
on whose anvil the great mammals
　　on their thinned migrations could be hammered.

'Do not hammer,' said the spirit people's leader,
　　when the One with Long Ears heard them
from their inland iglu,
　　　'when the whales are running.
Otherwise they will be frightened.'
　　So the shaman returned
with what the spirit people told him.
　　'I saw Pamiuguksaaq, the chief with a wolf's tail.
He was there with his wife, and Siutitaq
　　whose long ears pick up your taboo infractions.
And the spirits have already caught a whale.
　　They've got it to their iglu.
I almost stumbled on the flipper.'

So the hinge opened, swinging easily on whale oil
– finest lubrication – as it did, and neatly closed,
on feet and shoulders of those people in transition:

Europeans, Kanakas, Cape Verdeans, Americans,
　　Eskimo women and their *half-breed* children,
pushing at the door and drawing it behind them:
　　a division hinging the enclosure
that leaned out on the sea and back to long nights
　　filled with lamp-oil, hard tack,
boxed stores, journals, calculation,
　　talk and in trading jargon, *pani pani*[60],
south-seas whale-tongue, pidgin, Eskimo verb-stems
　　snapped off from their endings,
plots, drink, hairy knuckles, smooth copper forearms:
　　skin, wood and iron the constructive textures,

---

[60] sex

goods from the south and indoors reaching outwards,
    changing or exchanging, as they travelled, value and intrinsicality.

When I thought back to the children, I understood them better,
    or so I liked to think I saw them, as I'd tried to view myself
and antecedents in accretions and components
    were accumulated and recessant:
haphazard products of unstable histories,
    shedding separateness and animosity,
in mutual respect, confessing the limits,
    contemplating our conditioning
and reciprocating opaque versions.

I toyed with it now, what had swivelled
    and defined a doorway through which *aanas'* [61] mothers
had come working back then, as we now come too,
    through frames, days and thresholds,

but which let enter more than faces and shoulders,
    admitting, through the 19th century,
an *American present* to old America,[62]
    and which opened a space where,
backwards and forwards, epochs in accelerated,
    concentrated bundles shuttled,
the archaic and the modern grazing one another's edges,
    sometimes missing, and occasionally colliding.

---

[61] *aana:* grandmother   [62] 'American present': used to suggest both a verbal
tense and historical mood

Inter-rogation

This piece is independent of the previous narrative and merges visits I made to several old couples. Some of these were related to a man who had, as a result of tactless remark I had made, threatened to kill me.

'Then we have been wondering,' the woman said – she'd watched me as
    I'd stumped
 against the wind, flew back in its current and struggled at my door
with cardboard matches dying in the wind to thaw the padlock –
 'We have wondered what *sort of man* you are, or might be?'

'*What* sort?' I considered. *Not personal history, character and motivation.*
 She means 'kind' or 'species': my range, behaviour, patterns of feeding.
How I would mate. My migratory habits.

I'd found my way through her storm-shed passage.
 Beyond the wind, the air was weightless and yet textured.
The smell of oil rose from boot soles and mittens.
 There were stretched skins in frames on the freezer cabinet,
rifles and harpoon-shafts stacked against the ceiling.

I entered the strip lighting. There was a pile, apparently of blubber, on
    the table.
 Then, through the needles still unfrozen from my lashes, white
    bear-skin, maybe.
But *naagga*[63]: she was kneading, with a shamanistic heavy slapping, bread
    dough, bloated and elastic.
 '*Arrigaa!*[64]' I murmured, though not counting on a sandwich.
The grey dough writhed. It reared from the table, mute and silken.

'What sort of a man?' *Not psycho-history.*
 She grappled the dough and started to punch it.
'We've watched the way you hurry. What business is this with the old
    man's stories?
 You'll never understand them. They only make sense to us, in our
    language.'

---

[63]no [64]Good!

I sensed the wind her story carried of the white man's tapes, camera and
        notebooks,
    preying on her place, past, native property.
They came – back then – to take our language and our freedom.
    They built the school. Chased off the shamans.
Killed caribou and whales. Brought in whooping cough and measles. Jesus.
    Then: 'How come you aren't frightened living in the village?'

    I'm afraid of your brother,'
    I was frightened to answer.
    'All this month,
    he has been hunting me.
    I'm afraid of those coals
    that are his eyes.
    They have grilled me to cinders.

    The crystal of his skull
    has burned my retina.
    His voice, too's, found its way inside me.
    He keeps words in his neck:
    small, biting animals:
    they come out, half way, when I pass him,
    searching with their teeth
    and whiskers for me.

The dough submitted, ectoplasm palpitating only slightly, to her forearms.
    She slashed it in half and slotted each lump into glimmering bread tins,
and set them to prove on the oil-stove grating,
    stuffing with a woolen hat the ventilator flap to keep the draught off.

'We like it,' she said, switching, to the lee, her subject,
    'when you eat our meat. With your knife from the bone.
The way you *quaq*[65] Eat it with *uqsruq*[66]. . . You are even greedy.'
    'Yah, pretty hungry, maybe,' Suluk, the old husband, grunted,
and then gestured with his chin at some meat they hadn't finished.
    The woman slid a basin to me on the table.
'You better eat, ah?' he continued, without raising his head
    from the thing he was filing.
The split tusk sprayed his thumb with powder from the ivory,
    dust spiraling along the smoke flume of his Winston.

---

[65] Eat raw frozen meat   [66] blubber

I grappled for my portion among chilled crests of blubber,
    and lugged with my hand a fat piece from her basin.
'Where's your knife, then?' asked the woman sharply.
    I had not been prompt.
My hesitation, as though doubtful of their generosity, was rude and
        ungenerous.
    I drew out the knife from under my sweater and started to eat with
        canine gruntings.
Suluk glanced up to watch me feeding.
    They started to talk. Sketched out the logistics and particularities
in each of their stages through which a live seal became boiled seal meat.
    Niruvana had been out last Sunday on the north side,
where the ice had parted and had shot, in a single pond of water
    three seals, and dragged them all home on his sleds: no dogs, no skidoo.
'Hard time, that north-side-ice against the south wind,' Suluk murmured.
    'Lots of seal meat!' mused the woman.
Powder and ashes blew across the table.

It was merry to talk. Their voices were cheering.
    'So how long more you gonna stay round here,' she quizzed me.
'Don't you want to see your girl friend?'
    'Make little babies,' explained her husband.
I digested the focus: briefly now their subject.
    Not who I am but what, she's asking:
My texture. White flesh.
    But now penetrated and confused with real meat.

Fondling my knife and sweating through my hair,
    I started to arrange, like Scrabble in the smoke between us,
a legibly constructed answer.
    'It's hard to say where I might begin. I was born . . .'
My throatful of letters, -k and -q in dislocation, spilled, loosely corrupted.
    'As soon as your mother couldn't stand it!'
She half-stifled a laugh. Her husband grinned.
    His teeth were old ivory, twisted and gleaming.
They refracted the moment.
    Then he bit her laughter with them.
She said: 'We don't need a book about you,' — coughing.
    'Too much *sigrits*,[67]' murmured her husband.

---

[67] cigarettes

What *kind* of man had I come here to refashion?
    Now this was a subplot to the old man's stories.
Self as an item: to construe its nonsense and cut away some of it.

In a back-pack strung on my aching shoulder swung a cadaver of patches,
    the stitching unravelled and in flapping miscellaneous tassels.
Extruded through the scapula,
    I had tried to shake this from the globe's crest into European water,
and then to go roast, bald and naked on a north crust of the Arctic,
    reduce it in this crucible to powder,
cold-press, scour, distil and bleach it on the sea-ice.

                                            A naive project.

I'd jumped, as it passed towards his skinboat at the ice-edge,
    onto Piquk's dog-sled,
though he'd scarcely acknowledged the weight as he cantered
    along the solid inshore, whipped through the mush,
flown across the young stuff,
    and then through a defile of spiky ridges,
had lurched, banging the sled runners, up the sides of the gully,
    and had reached the calm black open water where the seals were feeding.

In that gully as we tumbled and regained momentum,
    I had clawed out something fussy, an old woolen from the inside of
        my stuffing.
My grip was paralyzed: but I'd grasped the worn-outness,
    spongey, flaccid and exsufflicate — and had hurled it to the foxes.

'Now that you've eaten, aren't you going to tell a story?'
    I was sleepy from meat and I'd dozed at the table.
The shirt I'd bought in Fairbanks was abrasive.
    They were testing me now there was real meat inside me.
Did *niqipiaq* ('real meat') in certain doses, convert one to Inupiaq ('a real
    person').

There were two dozen angles or so to this issue.
    I'd limned the polymorph on other but more loose occasions.
Counting on fingers below the table I registered a kind of order:

What was real (-*piaq*[68]) and what was -*nguaq* (opposite to -*piaq*)?
    Did *real* mean justified, elect and central to the pattern of their cosmos?
Or did reality connote a peculiar in-touchness:
    ancient subjectivity claiming deep connection to first principles,
back then in differentiation from the otherness of whales, caribou and
        marmots?

Aquppak, for instance, who had entered a whale's head,
    migrated north, returning next season to leave 'his' whale meat
        with the village.
Was he always *person*? *Human* whale soul? Whale-and-human blubber?
    How far did the shamans swing between 'genuine' and -*nguaq* condition,
when their souls became animals, or animals, reciprocally, became their
        person?
    Think of Kavisigluk, weary of humanity,
who one day left his family to join marmot *people*.
    When he dived in the burrow and Suuyuk called down to him,
Kavisigluk piped, in marmot language: 'I am staying! I'm staying!
    There are *people* down here. I have come to join them.'
Then there was Iqiasuaq, the lazy man, who ended his life as a solitary
        caribou.
    And Qipuagalautchiaq transforming to a polar bear.
His family watched him dive through the iglu entrance,
    bear claws scraping the polished floor planks.

Transformation! Metamorphosis! The manifest and latent juggled
    behind screens of imposition! Inter-species oscillation!
These were slipshod boundaries: blithe transgressions.
    The animals colluded. Spirits connived. -*piaq* (real) was jestingly fluid.

'I don't know any stories,' I murmured, turning half away,
    as already I knew decorum demanded, and gazed down, nebulously
        modest.
A silence followed. My heart beat heavily against my hot, rough shirt,
    as though first to scrape and finally to broil it.

'*Arrii!*' cried the woman, 'my bread gonna burnt!'
    Three loaves came out. They were perfect, smoking.
'*Arrigaa!*' smiled Suluk, driving his knife through a Smuckers tin-top[69],

---

[68] nominal suffix, as in *Inupiaq* = 'real person' or Eskimo.   [69] Smuckers: a make of
American jam.

136

To carve out some butter she twisted a can
which had melted and then frozen often.
　　　I'd eaten too much. This shift to a *tea* would make me vomit.

'You should know stories.'
　　　'Yah, he's told some stories.'
'Maybe-he-has-never-told-them,'
　　　Suluk went on, inching the suggestion to me.
'Just made something up. Just *saglu* (told lies) for a white man.'

If this was inquisition, it wasn't an unkindness;
　　　and if to affront, their motive was knowledge.
Besides, I was younger. And youth, while lovely in the comparative way,
　　　was fraught with events and too elastic:
not to be trusted with collective history,
　　　cycles of memory, temporal concatenations, past and present,
the imbricated texture of relations, with their knit and crises.
　　　To algebrize would be-to-be a cannibal, and eat the elders.
The aged mastodon had claimed me. I was his grandson.
　　　Together we formed *aapa-giik*: 'father-and-another':
a compound folkloristic 'person' idea: the *aapa*-noun a magical curmudgeon,
　　　and the orphan *-giik,* an adjunct-without-kin,
the poor boy a mere suffix: the two unified in isolation on the margin
　　　of some nameless village run by married folk with proper children.

The Bellman's Story

I was snowbound in my cabin one Saturday in March when six girls rolled in and asked for a story they'd heard I had told to other people in the village. The following tale, more or less as I spoke it, is in affectionate mimesis of Asatchaq's stories as translated into village English. Most of the story's action takes place in Fairbanks where I had lived before this trip. Booster (Many Press 1976; see also 'At Kunuyaq's' above) is a game of divination containing 150 apothegms and mottos. I had written this the previous winter and played it with young men in the village.

Uqaluktuagniaqtuna! I'm going to tell a story.
I told this one to Piquk, Cool Daddy and Konrad.
The story is a true one. It happened in Fairbanks.
The story's about me. I lived down town. Near the log cabins.
Third Avenue-*mission*[70]. A small house. Old.
It was built in the forties. I don't know who made it.
Five of us lived there.
We shared the rent and sometimes ate together.
I was getting ready for my trip to Tikigaq.
I went to college in the mornings. I went to learn Inupiaq at college.
A white man taught us. Larry. A good teacher.
He really knows Inupiaq.
After I ate lunch I studied in the library. I worked on Inupiaq.
That's how I lived. I'd saved some money.
It wasn't enough.
My cheque would come in New Year, only.
I needed the money to pay Asatchaq for stories.
I needed more money for rent and travel.
So I looked for a job. There were several in Fairbanks.
Most of my friends had jobs on the pipeline.
The jobs I could get were in hotels and restaurants.
So I went to *Jake's Cabin*.
It's down by the river.
I went and talked to Jakey. Jakey was a white man.
'OK,' said Jake, 'you can start this evening.
Get here at six. You can work in the kitchen.'
So I got there at six. And they taught me to make pizza.

---

[70] The locative enclitic, 'in'.

Lots of people came to eat. That kitchen was busy.
We rolled out the dough and cut it in circles.
There was lots of cheese. It was in bits and it came in boxes.
We threw on cheese and mushrooms, meat and pepper.
The orders came on paper through a window in the kitchen.
It was hot in the kitchen. There were four other cooks.
All five of us were white boys:
but all of *them* were Jehovah's Witnesses.
All they talked about was Jesus witnessing.
I didn't join in. When they asked me my religion I said nothing.
'You must be some pagan.' That's what they told me.

So in my breaks I walked down to the river.
   The banks were muddy, the weeds were dying.
The weeds and the reeds had frozen already: bending, broken.
   I'd been here with my girl friend earlier that autumn.
We sat by the water and watched the migrations.
   Ducks and geese coming down from the Arctic.
That place on the river was no good for fishing.
   To do any fishing you had to go up river.
There are moose there too. In a couple of weeks,
   hunters who had licences would go up river.
There are plenty of moose there feeding by the water.

You asked me about Ernie. Ernie didn't have a license.
Ernie shot one.
Went to prison three weeks for it.
That moose had come into his garden.
Ernie and Kora had a garden.
They lived high on a ridge, twelve miles out of Fairbanks.
They'd bought some land and built a house.
Kora did the garden in the summer.
Lots of white folks like to eat vegetables. They can't help it.
They fenced in the garden to protect it from rabbits.
But that moose just stepped through it.
It ate most of their vegetables in just five minutes.

Ernie went in and fetched his rifle.
He walked right up to that moose in his garden
and point blank shot it.
The moose died right there. Just one shot killed it.

It fell down in the carrots and they skinned it:
cut up the body and put it in their freezer.
They kept their freezer in the garage.

Then a man called Owl Claws called the State Troopers.
Owl Claws was a white man. Big one.
He wore owl's feet on a string.
He hung them round his neck,
like old timers here in Tikigaq.
'There's a dead moose up the Ridge,' he told those troopers.
'Somebody has shot it. He didn't have a licence.'

The troopers drove up in a four-wheel-drive pickup.
They came and opened Kora's freezer.
She and Ernie had butchered the whole animal.
They'd wrapped the pieces in freezer paper.
When the Troopers saw the meat, they said:
'Is this moose meat?' Kora was crying.
'Is this meat moose meat?' the troopers asked Kora.
'It was eating our garden. We'll have nothing to live on.'
So they took away the meat.
Kora and Ernie were left with nothing.

Then Ernie and Owl Claws started to quarrel.
First they quarrelled on the moose meat.
Then they quarrelled about fences.
Ernie chartered a plane and flew to Valdez.
He went to Valdez: at the end of the pipeline.
The pipeline people were selling equipment they had finished with.[71]
People flew down to buy it at auctions.
Ernie flew down with his cheque-book.
He bought three hundred fence posts,
a tank for getting the salt out of water,
and a dome that came in five thousand pieces.
The dome came in pieces. Polystyrene.
I saw those pieces. Ernie never built it.
As part of the deal Ernie had to take some other things:
sugar dispensers, restaurant trays and salt and pepper shakers.
Thirty dozen. More than three thousand.

---

[71] Anachronistic detail. The events here took place the year before pipeline completion.

140

I saw them myself a year or so later.
The packing had burst:
the ground by their garage was covered with salt and pepper shakers.
Both kinds.
But they couldn't use them.

Ernie rented a plane and brought the whole lot back to Fairbanks.
He unloaded on his land,
and the very next day his house burned down.
They lost the house, their books and records, clothes and pictures.
They moved into their garage where they kept their freezer.

So they started to keep rabbits.
They grew vegetables all summer.
All summer and fall they bottled and canned them.
They ate nothing but rabbits: with peas, beans, beets, and lettuce,
carrots and tomatoes.
They got money on insurance,
and Ernie grew *qaaq*[72] which he sold in Fairbanks.

Ernie had been to school in Boston.
He'd studied the aurora.
He went to the Antarctic.
It was cold like here there, maybe even colder.
He spent two years studying aurora.
He lived down there with lots of other scientists.
All they knew, those men, was scientific knowledge.
They lived in isolation.
They all went crazy.
They became little boys.
They pretended to be trains.
They ran through their housing and made engine noises.
They made railroad schedules.
They talked engine language.
They pretended they were aeroplanes and whales and penguins.
Maybe Ernie, too, went crazy with them.
He wrote to a friend to send him *qaaq* seeds.
The seeds took six months to come from Berkeley.
Ernie planted them in pots. He grew bushes in a window.

---

[72] Marijuana

It's light there all summer.
Their summer is our winter: their winter is our summer.

When Ernie tried his *qaaq* out, it was strong and tasty.
He got really *qanga*.[73]
He packed some up and sent it to America.
His friends in Berkeley got *qaaq* from the Antarctic.
Then another plane flew down. Ernie went to New Zealand.
He gave up studying.
He could have been a big professor.
He came to Alaska. He built a house with Kora.
Three years it took them.
When it burned down, they slept in the garage and lived on rabbits.
Then they got tired of it.
'Let's go to New Zealand!'
That's how they planned it.

When he came out of prison,
Ernie found that Owl Claws had taken some land away.
Owl Claws had moved the fence posts Ernie had planted.
When Ernie saw what Owl Claws had started,
he loaded his shot gun and got on his dozer.
Kora ran after him.
'Don't shoot him, Ernie! Don't shoot, Ernie!'
Kora ran ahead. She threw herself down.
She lay in the mud between Ernie and Owl Claws.
Ernie stopped the machine.
And Kora made Owl Claws move the fence back.
It was Kora who made him. Just by talking.
That's how they lived. They quarrelled with their neighbour.
They planned to leave Fairbanks: go to New Zealand.
Still they lived on in their garage, eating rabbits.

I was working on a late shift, making Jakey's pizzas.
But I couldn't get on with those Jehovah's Witnesses.
Those Witnesses boys had a kind of leader.
His name was Orville.
One night Orville got me by the pizza oven.
He tried to make me come to their meetings.

---

[73] stoned

I told him I wouldn't.
This made him angry. He said:
'You'll roast! You'll roast in hell just like that pizza!'
He beat his knuckles on the oven.
So I went to the boss. I told Jake I was leaving.
'Okay,' said Jakey. 'Can't say I blame you.'

Now I looked for work again.
I walked through Fairbanks.
The snow had started.
It was almost evening.
I came to a hotel they called *The Trapper*.
It's a big log building near the edge of Fairbanks.
I went in. To the desk.
'I'm looking for a job.
A job for the evenings.'
The woman at the desk said:
'We've got an opening for junior bellman.
'What's a bellman?' I asked.
'Bellman's a bellboy. He sits in the lobby.
When guests come in, the bellman carries their bags to their bedroom.
It's three bucks an hour. Tips are extra.
I'll introduce you to the senior bellman.'

The senior bellman was high school student.
A boy called Rick. Some people called him Ricky.
Rick took me to a cupboard.
It was full of bow-ties, vests and towels.
The corridor was empty.
The corridor smelled of vacuum cleaning.
Rick gave me a bow tie and a waistcoat.
We each took a towel.
'You can wear your own pants. Black pants. White shirt.
And this vest and bow-tie.'

Next day I went to the Salvation Army.
I bought a shirt and blue cord trousers.
They fitted me well.
I've got them here. I still wear those trousers.
And this is the shirt I bought that morning.
It was made in Montana.

The work wasn't hard.
I started at six and worked until midnight.
I sat in the lobby and waited for guests.
To pick up their cases.
There weren't very many.
The next evening I brought my Inupiaq homework.
I sat and did my homework in the lobby:
I sat opposite the desk.
The lady did crosswords.
I did my homework:

Tautukpigu: 'Am I seeing it?' Tautukkiga: 'I am seeing it.'
Qilakpisigu: 'Are we knitting it?' Qilakkikput: 'We are knitting it.'
Akkuaqpiun: 'Did you just catch it?' Akkuagiga: 'I just caught it.'

That's the sort of homework Larry gave us.
I learned lots of words and some of the bits that go inside words:
How *piqsiq + niaq + tuq* makes *piqsigniaqtuq*
(There will be blowing snow.)
How *aqpat + nit + lutik* makes *aqpannillutik*
(Because the two of them did not run.)
How *itqutchiq + niaq + tugut* makes *itqutchigniaqtugut*
(We will breakfast.)

I wrote out my homework for class next morning.
'You getting some smarts?' the woman asked me.
She was someone to talk to.
'I'm not too sure. I'm trying to learn this language.'
'What language is it?' the woman asked me.
I told her I was learning some Inupiaq.
'Never heard of it,' she said.
'It's the Eskimo's language.'
'I've lived in Alaska these fifteen years,' the woman said,
'and young man, I assure you, they don't have a language.'
'Look, this is their language.' I showed her some typed pages.
'These words are Eskimo.' And I spoke them to her.
'That's just nonsense,' said the woman.
'No-one talks like that. I don't get a word of it.'
'What are these words then?'
'Some smart-assed professor's made those words up.
You've been taken for a ride, son. Go and earn a proper living.'

'But this is my work,' I tried explaining.
'There's this old man. He knows a lot of stories.
I'm going to his village. When I've learned his language,
it'll help me translate them.'
'A drinker, I reckon, spinning you a snow job.
That's all they're good for. Go down Second Avenue.
All those Eskies know's the inside of a bottle.
And where's their dollar coming from?
A fat monthly cheque from Social security. Out of *my* taxes.'

Most nights I worked alone.
But sometimes on a week-end shift the head bellman came too.
His job was to train me.
He showed me how to raise Old Glory and then bring it down again.
He told me the Stars and Stripes must never touch the ground.
If the flag touched the ground it would lose its power.
Its power would drain out. The earth would harm it.
So one afternoon we went outside.
The flagpole stood opposite the hotel coffee shop.
People sat behind the windows, eating and smoking.
Outside it was cold. It had started snowing.
A store sign opposite read: 'Parking for Gulls'.
Gulls was a store for vacuum cleaners.
I thought that sign was funny. *Nauyaq. Nauyaaluk.*[74]
I tried translating the sign into Inupiaq.
But Rick wouldn't listen. He stood to attention.
He saluted Old Glory and undid the lanyard.
The flag started running. It rattled down the flag post.
'Catch it bellman!' But the it fell on the gravel.
'Shithead! Asshole!' the head bellman shouted.
'You did that on purpose!' 'I'm sorry,' I told him.

Then I had to learn to fill the noticeboard with letters.
They had conferences at *Trappers*.
They had to be shown on the hotel notice board.
The board stood on an easel.
It was lined with black velvet.
Rick gave me a box full of white plastic letters.
You picked out letters and stuck them in the velvet.

---

[74] Inupiaq, 'common gull' + *–aaluk*, 'big, old' = 'full grown *nauyaq*'.

Rick had all the day's announcements in his pocket.
That's when I started to quarrel with Ricky.
We quarrelled over spelling.
There were conferences and meetings that I had to spell.
Meetings of dentists and business people.
Rick told me I'd spelled 'Annual Conference' wrong.
I'd used up the *n*'s. I should keep them for later.
I told him I was an English teacher. I needed those *n*-s.
Both words needed two of them.
'Oh yeah? Catch these spellings!'
And he shook my sentences onto the carpet and made me start over.

The next day it froze.
The snow turned to ice in the motel courtyard.
I'd gone to the bar to fill some orders.
I was crossing the yard with a tray of cocktails.
There was ice in the courtyard. I was trying to be careful.
Then a big Dodge roared in through the archway.
It was going at 30.
It was Ricky, the head bellman.
He saw me in his headlights, but he didn't stop driving.
I was straight in his path.
I was carrying those cocktails.
There was nowhere else to go. I jumped into the doorway.
I got rid of the drinks tray.
There were two Bloody Marys.
They froze on his windshield.
The ice hit my waistcoat.
'Nice shot teacher!' Ricky shouted.
I guess he'd been drinking.
I went back to the bar to get more Bloody Marys.
I thought I'd be fired.
I ordered a Jack Daniels.
I ordered another.
But no-one said nothing.

I filled a new tray and added some peanuts.
A man and woman had come down from a pipeline camp
for rest and recreation and had ordered cocktails.
I got in the lift and took their drinks up.
When I got to their door, I could hear that they were high on
            something,

cocaine maybe. They *kuyaked* shrilly, sexed up, giggling.
I didn't want to interrupt them.
I rattled the ice in their highball glasses
and set down the tray in the empty passage.

It was seven at night and I'd just sat down to my Eskimo homework
when a string quartet arrived from the airport.
It was the Guarnieris. I knew they were coming.
They'd flown in from Osaka. On their way to New York City.
They were playing at the U tomorrow. Haydn, Mozart and Dvorák.
I'd bought a ticket. I had leave for next evening.
I was upset still from my quarrel with the bellman.
I stood up. I was shaking. I was going to meet them.

They checked in. I'd seen them ten years back in London.
'Come to give the folks some good ole tunes?' said the woman at
    reception.
'Which'v youse guys does lip-synch?'
They were quiet men, friendly. They chatted to the lady.
I picked up their bags. They carried their own instruments.

I mooned past their bedrooms late that evening.
    Michael Tree on the viola intoned 'Seid ihr nicht der Schwanen-
        dreher?'
Steinhardt the leader dreamed through a Szymanowski *Legend*,
    Dalley and Soyer bowed darkly into the Kodaly duo.

After the concert I went to say hello with Larry.
'Our hotel porter!' exclaimed Arnold Steinhardt, 'what a range of
    interests!'
We talked for a while. Arnie asked us at once about Inupiaq.

I wanted to say: 'I'll never learn properly. That's for virtuosi.
    You on the fiddle and Larry here, in language pyrotechnics.
We poets stagger through creation's bits and pieces: farceurs, flaneurs,
        butterflies:
    we browse figments and fragments – ultimate or rudimentary –
and try to fuse these, in some coalition of a relative and intermediate samjna,[75]
        with a circumstantial and haphazard colour and our own chaotic rhythms.

---

[75] Pali: 'limited human perception' as opposed to insight

You work technically, with consciousness broader than we'll ever stretch to
  in our self-enclosure,
We speak from solo ipse and non-knowledge: one eye half open to relative truth
  and the semi-unconscious:
  the other beating the corpuscular muddle thrown up on our eye-lids by
  indecipherable photons:
  images from half-truth crystallised in sacred fear at having the
  chutzpah to approach sublime kingdoms.'

I walked out late, and stood beneath Orion.
  The crusted spruce looked dwarfish and sullen.
'How many kingdoms know us not?' the words came.[76]
  'We must match their indifference with burning solicitude.
This must be the motif of my work here.
  Have courage and be tranquil,' I scolded myself, shrinking.
'Acknowledge you may learn, but most likely achieve nothing.'

Logistics took over.
  Worries about packing, clothes, equipment, plane flights, money:
what to do about polar bears and rabid foxes, trichanosis.
  'What good's a book?
A single tile, like one of Ernie's geodesic dome slabs
  in the heap that welters round the world tree.
What matters is now: not some test,
  nor yet the crucible of ice and darkness:
but whether I can rub along,
  live graciously sans greed or competition:
hunting in peace like a Tikigaq hunter:
  this project a wrought exercise and tactic:
walking any lay-out given, then tactfully leaving
  to contemplate the structure of the stories' cosmos,
the design of this ancient people's thinking:
  their shape in the context of a world imagination.'

The *taaqsipaks*[77] arrived three nights later.
Two sets of two-tones lowered from a taxi:
tan-and-white spats,
and pair of squarer black and white deals.
I recognised the spat man. Name of Arnie:

---

[76] I was preoccupied at the time with Pascal's exclamation which complements 'These spaces frighten me.'   [77] black people; literally, 'grown dark'.

148

Arnie the pusher, not Arnie *Guarnieri*.
I'd seen Arnie (1) at the U.S. Dewline base at Barrow.
I'd gone there with Hanky, an education salesman.
Barrow was dry, so we'd gone for a drink.
The barman was English.
A technician from Yorkshire who did radar systems.
The men at the base all belonged to a club.
The bar was part of it, with a cage in the corner
for a Go-Go dancer. They paid subscriptions,
and took it in turns to serve behind the counter.
Drinks were quite cheap: beer 15 cents, $1 for spirits.
Then Arnie arrived.
He wanted a bottle, but the man from Yorkshire wouldn't serve him.
Arnie hadn't paid his bar bill. He refused to pay it.
The man from Yorkshire didn't mince words.

Arnie, he said, was a son-of-a-bitch twister:
all he knew was skiving and scrounging.
He told him not look for favours
because he (the boffin) gave nary-a-toss for the junk
that Arnie fixed the boys with.
'So gimme a drink,' said Arnie smiling.
'Go fuck yourself backwards' the barman whispered,
'or I'll sling your black guts round the radar mushroom.'
Words continued. But after each of the Yorkshireman's *fuck-offs*,
Arnie leaned forward on the bar and whispered:
'*Eat mah shee*-yet. Eat *mah* shee-yet.' Smiling but emphatic.

So here was Arnie, five months later, checking into the Fairbanks *Trapper*,
green jacket, pink flares, cuff links in diced abalone.
Cyril, Arnie's partner, dressed in black and orange.
'*Hey, bellboh*, take these boxes, don't leave them in the wet,' said Arnie.
It was snowing in the courtyard.
They had nine cases, thereabout, including some open cardboard boxes.
It looked as though they'd been through Pay n' Save
snapping up knick-knacks as they passed them.
Arnie was still cool.
But Cyril, the partner, was restless and nervy.
He rocked on his heel, kept one hand in his jacket.

I started to lead them through the corridor.
My trolley was groaning.
'Don't drop those, son,' said Cyril (in orange),
'we don't want bad herb on the carpet.'
'You want bad herb, man?' said Arnie.
'I just roll in and visit this cat in his crib and he laid 20 on me.'
I'd packed the trolley high and clumsy
so the luggage tottered and the wheels sank in the carpet.
To make matters worse I got lost, and the doors of the lift stuck.
We stepped out for a moment to see where we'd got to,
and the lift ran off with their trolley-full of cases.
When it came back, the doors got stuck open.
Bored and frightened, I tried making small-talk.
The conversation zigzagged up to Barrow.
'How's your friend at the bar who wanted your tripes
for the radar mushroom?' I dangerously asked him.
We were miles from reception, in a maze of bedrooms.
Arnie froze the jive-ass component.
'This bellboy is something!' I was flattered.
He pulled out two wallets in burgundy and crocodile.
Each cheque book had a different name and P.O. number.
'I'm *boss*,' he said darkly. 'Both of me is.'
'You crazy?' Cyril stabbed in, 'This guy could —— '
whipping out a small revolver.
The gun was tiny. I thought he'd picked it up from Woolworths,
like the stuff in his boxes from Pay n' Save and Super Rexall.

Then Cyril spun the chamber and I saw the hammer.
'That gat: don't sap me with it,' I managed to stammer from
                Raymond Chandler.
'Who is this guy?' snapped Cyril in a whisper.
'Some punk. I don't know,' muttered Arnie, half-frowning.
Cyril marched round by the open lift cage flourishing his pistol.
He wasn't pleased, unlike the fellow in Mae West's, to see me.
'This cat. I don't believe it! Stuck here, and he knows your . . .
This guy's getting fired, I'm telling you . . .'
'But not that gun I hope,' I tittered.
Both of them were stoned, drunk, out of it, just then I realised,
and the Barrow encounter jarred their memories,
collapsed and drifting, in the usual marijuana tangle.
I slipped round the edge and came out as bellhop with their luggage
                trolley.

The rest of that evening I spent running errands.
Arnie and Cyril had jugs of vodka.
I shuttled them ice, I changed their glasses.
The glasses were wrong. They needed more ash-trays.
They wanted cigarettes from Turkey.
I ran out to get them on 5th Avenue.
When I got back, they had two girls with them:
Tiffany and Sunshine, both in underwear.
Arnie gave me a dollar, a joint and a vodka.
This was stingy but fun. I enjoyed my evening.

Next night, quite late, Arnie called reception.
They wanted me up there.
'This room's no use. We need a new one.'
I ran upstairs and found them sweating.
They'd packed already.
I called down to confirm the booking.
'It's someone on their tail!' the lady whispered.
She was excited.
To Arnie it was just a game still:
'You want to earn a *real* tip this time, bellman?'
He leaned back in his chair and fished up his wallet.
He took out five bills and laid them on the carpet.
'You move us in five minutes, bellboy: and you get *these*.'
They were new, crisp centuries.
I took up the challenge. I wanted those dollars.
I might have done it if I'd known my way, and not dropped too
                    many boxes.
I hurried the corners. The two *taaqsipaks* followed.
The trolley wouldn't run straight.
Cyril slung a rolled-up copy of the evening paper with his pistol in it.
Arnie sang the minutes. He knew I couldn't.

We had one more meeting. I'd told them about *Booster*.
That's my book of questions.
Cousin Lazarus and Piquk have played it.
It's a book of funny answers.
The men wanted to see it.
So I took them the dice, and mottos in typescript.
'Will the Man get us?' That was Cyril's question.
Cyril shook the dice and threw Bell-Orange-Cherry.

Dice rattled on his pistol.
'That's the empty combination,' I told him.
'There's no motto for it.
Lay down your gun if you want an answer.'
Cyril liked the hierophantic posture.
He did as I told him, and shriven, he threw clearer.

It was Orange-Orange-Cherry. I read out his answer:
Someone with clear eyes is tired of watching out for you. Cultivate self-love.
'What's that mean?' asked Cyril, excited by flashes of his mother in
               Chicago.
'That's for *you* to figure out,' said Arnie.
'If we play properly,' I said, 'you get four answers.'
'No, no. No time,' said Arnie, impatient. 'Give me my turn.'
'What's your question?'
'This is my question: 'How come I'm here now?''
He scattered the dice and threw up Plum-Lemon-Orange:
'*The texture of all flesh from Mae West to the Eskimos is one,*' said *Booster*.
'Oh,' said Arnie.
'Let me give you the companion motto. Number 84.
It's one of my favourites:
'*Extreme alternatives. Untidy circus of emotion:*
the glamorous equipment is exhausted by display.
or:
The whips and harnesses rot in the night dew with neglect.'
'I'll meditate on that,' said Arnie.
He wrote down his answer in his crocodile-skin cheque book.
'Huh,' said Cyril.
That's where I left them.

At the end of the telling, the six girls got up and left the cabin.
'Goodbye,' I said.
But Inuit don't say goodbye.
They just walk off in the silence.

Tom Lowenstein worked in the Inuit village of Tikigaq (Point Hope, Alaska) in the 1970s and 80s where he recorded narratives and songs with community elders. He recently completed *Ultimate Americans: a history of 19th century contact between Point Hope Inuit and Euro-Americans*. He lives in London with his wife and two daughters.

www.ingramcontent.com/pod-product-compliance
Lightning Source LLC
Chambersburg PA
CBHW020246290326
41930CB00038B/411